Membership
Marketing

Membership Marketing

EDITED BY

Susan Nicolais, CAE

ASAE Membership Section

asae | american society of association executives

WASHINGTON, D.C.

American Society of Association Executives
1575 I Street, NW
Washington, DC 20005
Phone: (202) 626-2723
Fax: (202) 408-9634
E-mail: books@asaenet.org

George E. Moffat, Publisher
Linda Munday, Director of Book Publishing
Anna Nunan, Book Acquisitions Coordinator
Jennifer Moon, Production Coordinator
Cover and interior design by Troy Scott Parker, Cimarron Design

This book is available at a special discount when ordered in bulk quantities. For information, contact the ASAE Member Service Center at (202) 371-0940.

A complete catalog of titles is available on the ASAE Web site at
www.asaenet.org/bookstore

Library of Congress Cataloging-in-Publication Data

Membership marketing / Susan Nicolais, editor.
        p. cm. — (Core competencies in membership management)
    Includes bibliographical references.
    ISBN 0-88034-164-5
        1. Association marketing. I. Nicolais, Susan. II. Series.

    HF5415.1252 .M45 2000
    060'.68'8—dc21
                                                                00-026163

Printed in the United States of America.
10 9 8 7 6 5 4 3 2 1

Contents

Preface

SEVERAL YEARS AGO, THE ASAE Membership Section Council undertook the review of the existing printed materials available for membership professionals. As we were going through the process, it became evident that to truly address the needs of those in membership we would first need to have a thorough understanding of the many "things" that are part of a membership professional's job.

Thus began our quest to identify and refine the membership body of knowledge. Through small group meetings, focus groups, and teleconferences, many membership section members participated in this quest and made it a reality. The result is a living document that changes and grows along with the membership profession. The body of knowledge will be used to guide the Membership Section Council in identifying educational and publication needs of section members.

From the membership body of knowledge the section council was able to identify the areas that needed updated publications. The initial thought was to create one book to address all of the areas identified in the body of knowledge. After careful consideration, it was decided to produce a series of three handbooks that will address functional areas of the membership profession rather than one all encompassing book. The handbooks will cover membership marketing, membership operations, and member services. Producing three separate books allows us to move forward in a more timely manner and also gives us the flexibility in updating the material as changes occur.

Membership Marketing is the first handbook in the series produced. It is a compilation of the expertise of many authors, reviewers, and editors. These individuals are committed to the membership profession and gave selflessly of their time to help others grow in the profession. I would like to thank each of them for making this book a reality. Special thanks go to Melissa Angerman, Cathy Breden, Suzanne Bowman, Kristin Ekanger, Diane Feirman, Julie Koch, Stacey Riska, April Shaughnessy, Cindy Sheridan, Lorili Toth and Johanna Vanarsdall for reviewing the chapters and providing insight and guidance to the authors.

– Susan Nicolais, CAE

CHAPTER ONE

Association Research

Arlene Farber Sirkin and Miriam T. Meister, CAE

MANY SUCCESSFUL ASSOCIATIONS value market research activities. They have learned an important lesson from the for-profit sector: Good market research is an investment for successful marketing of membership and member services. The for-profit sector does it—not because it's the right thing to do—because it's the smart thing to do.

Some associations, however, struggle over the proper role for market research in their organizations. They do not understand the benefits of good market research or have relied exclusively on the input of a few members—such as their board or executive committee members—who often are not representative of the membership as a whole. When associations bundled all their products and services into membership dues, market research was not as much of an issue. Now that many associations have unbundled their member services and products and depend more on a stable or growing membership as well as on nondues revenue, market research is critical to success.

Market research offers an association many benefits for strategic planning, membership development and retention, and product and service development and marketing. Market research can provide a solid fact base for the association's decision making and can send a strong message to the association's membership (and prospective members) that the leadership is committed to meeting member needs and expectations. Ideally, if the association effectively researches and gives members what they want, the increased value should lead to increased member retention.

But associations must be realistic about what they can achieve directly through market research. Market research is not in and of itself a miracle cure that can immediately turn around an association's image and positioning, strategic planning, membership growth, or product mix. Rather, it is a decision-support tool that, together with an understanding of political needs and judicious use of common sense, will help the association make better decisions and use of an association's limited resources.

Associations should avoid setting unrealistic goals for specific research efforts, such as "x%" growth in new membership or specific retention goals. They should understand that regular market research strengthens their underlying decisions and leads to better results over time. The association's leadership—both volunteer and staff—must be willing to commit the necessary resources (including staff, budget, data systems, and fees for experienced researchers—internal or external) to do proper market research.

A change in an association's external environment frequently drives some associations to consider using market research. External environmental changes may include increased competition from other nonprofit entities or challenges from for-profit entities that are adversely affecting the association's image, positioning, or membership and marketing success. New competition to the industry may pose common challenges and issues for the association's members.

Each association operates under different circumstances; these circumstances determine the type of market research needed. One association may use market research to identify trends in the industry, profession, or cause served by the association and assess their short- and long-range effects on the association's membership, markets, and products. Another association may be looking for a more broad-based identification and evaluation of member needs followed by a more in-depth assessment of specific areas, such as education resources, meetings, advocacy efforts, member services, technology, and communications.

An inventory of the areas in which market research can help associations is nearly inexhaustible. Some common types of research used by associations and the benefits they achieve through these efforts are summarized in Figure 1-1.

FIGURE 1-1

Research Methods Used by Associations

Type of Research Conducted	Potential Uses of Research Findings
Member (and customer) needs assessment	• Fine-tune current product offerings • Develop new products and services • Improve and speed fulfillment processes and customer service • Assess how well the association is meeting the needs of each key member segment and identify areas where improvement is needed
Assessment of new products, services, or improvements to existing products and services	• Provide decision support for improvements to existing products and services • Provide decision support for development, delivery, pricing, and marketing communication for new products and services
Evaluation of member expectations and the association's performance in specific program or product areas (e.g., conferences, publications, advocacy, governance, communications, needs fulfillment, use of technology)	• Provide decision support for determining improvements needed in program or product areas • Provide a report card for leadership as it determines allocation of association resources
Identification and assessment of marketplace trends and evaluation of member support of potential strategy directions for the association	• Provide a valuable component for the association's environmental scan and fact base for decision support for its strategic planning efforts by providing facts
Member satisfaction of benefits and services offered, with their level of quality, usefulness, and the quality of customer service in delivering them	• Identify member segments most satisfied with the association and those least satisfied (and therefore vulnerable to nonrenewal of membership) • Identify product, program, and member service areas that may need improvement or better communication of their benefits to members
Assessment of the association's image and positioning (i.e., how members, prospects, and others view the association relative to other entities and competitors in the marketplace—both nonprofit and for-profit)	• Provide decision support for membership and communications by identifying ways to better position and communicate the activities, programs, and benefits of the association to its key constituencies and to establish the branding of the association

Continues next page

Type of Research Conducted	Potential Uses of Research Findings
New member survey	• Identify the relative importance of various benefits, services, and other factors that motivate the membership decision
Defector research and analysis	• Identify the relative influence certain factors have on the membership renewal decision and helps the association make needed changes or improvements
Member benefit and market segmentation analysis	• Identify member segments that may be under-served in terms of member services, benefits, communications, networking, etc.
Rejector research and analysis	• Identify factors (or barriers) influencing the rejection of association membership by eligible prospects
Technology status	• Identify status of membership on the communication continuum—do they have or want electronic communication? • Identify a census of members to self-identify preferred mode of communication from the association (e-mail, fax, hardcopy)
Restructuring and reorganization	• Identify new models for providing maximum value to members at headquarter and multiple levels
Sponsorship research	• Identify the benefits to business partners (vendors and suppliers) who seek to maximize their contribution to and benefit from the association
Industry- or profession-related research (cost studies, salary surveys, etc.)	• Provide, through reports, a valuable service to the association's members as well as potential nondues revenues

Types of Association Market Research and Their Uses

Where to Start—Secondary Research

Before an association decides to initiate new primary research, it should conduct a thorough inventory of existing internal resources—association archives, staff files, and current data sources—to identify existing information that may be relevant to the specific issue(s) to be studied.

In some cases, associations discover that there is no need for new research because other areas of the association or external sources (such as the government, academia, or others in the industry) have conducted similar studies. In other cases, these secondary research resources may provide only partial answers to the issues at hand. In these cases, research dollars can focus on the questions that remain unanswered, thereby avoiding duplicating research efforts.

Each association should have one office, person, or department responsible for collecting and maintaining copies of all internally provided research. When existing research is gathered, senior staff often are surprised at how much information is already out there. Especially in large associations with decentralized marketing, one unit may not know of relevant research that another part of the association has created and filed away. There may be a surprising number of instances where no one on staff has a copy of a study that was done within the last 2–3 years mainly because of staff turnover.

To determine whether existing research adequately addresses the association's current needs, the association should decide whether the study's objectives are relevant to those needs, whether the study's quality ensures its reliability, and whether the data produce credible results. A research project may have been conducted so poorly or may have had such a low response rate that it is invalid.

The association should examine the sampling methods that were used for the research (e.g., what market or member segments were included in the sample, how was the sample selected, and what is the size of the sample relative to the total size of the market); how the data were compiled (e.g., are segments of the market you wish to study included in the original study); and whether there was a sufficient and credible response to the survey that would ensure the data developed are scientifically reliable and whether there was any other source of bias that would invalidate the results.

Internal Sources

Membership databases can be a valuable source for secondary research, especially if the data can be retrieved by specific market segment and other key demographics, such as age, gender, employment information, educational degree, special interest areas, reasons for joining, length of membership, use of association products and services, and participation in association activities and leadership. If an association's database is not capable of storing the basic data needed, the association should consider a new and upgraded system. In most cases, this will save money and time by providing opportunities to segment and use target marketing efforts.

The association can use these data to assess which market segments have the best membership growth and to identify the market segments that have developed fewer members. A member database also can help the association build member profiles and help the leadership understand each segment and its specific needs (e.g., the most active members who wish to give back to their profession, new career professionals that may have special educational needs, and baby boomer or post-boomer members whose hectic lives require creative approaches to enhance member communications and participation). In several instances, associations use these databases to determine if they are missing opportunities to better serve specific groups, such as the international sector, that could add to the bottom line.

Prospect databases can be helpful, especially if the association identifies and tracks its membership and products by source code. At a minimum, they can help identify market segments most likely to consider membership, purchase products, or participate in meetings and educational seminars and identify the most or least productive sources of new and retained members. Often, a new member source, such as an annual conference, brings in a lot of new members, but most members gained leave in a year or two. Once that hole has been identified, the association can focus on specific measures to improve retention of members gained through that particular new member source.

Member service databases can be gold mines of information, especially for identifying purchase and use patterns by member or market segments over a period of time—for example, over the past three to five years. As the association considers developing new products and services, assessing how well similar products and services have fared over the years and evaluating how profitable similar products or lines have been with the member segments that form its core market can be helpful. The best prospects can be used to provide feedback to help develop and market the new product.

Anecdotal evidence of member interest in a specific product or member service can be helpful when evaluating a new product. Anecdotal evidence may be derived from direct queries received at the headquarters office about availability of a product or service or may come from review of reports by field staff over a certain period. Many associations have an information central or customer service center where staff record reasons for each call. This information is compiled and developed into a report provided to membership and to staff in other key areas. Some associations schedule visits by senior staff and volunteer leaders to member sites. Written reports of these visits can provide helpful anecdotal evidence of member needs, interests, and opinions, which should be shared with other staff. Often these anecdotes, as well as verbatim comments from surveys, lead to ideas for new products and services.

It is important to know if similar products and services offered in the past have encountered delivery or other customer service problems, or if recent marketing efforts to key member segments have been unsuccessful. This type of secondary data can help the association determine how best to use available (and often limited) research and marketing dollars.

External Sources

Before embarking on new primary research, external sources of secondary research should be explored to avoid duplicating existing information. The best starting point for many associations is their component groups and related organizations. National associations should inventory what their state, local, regional, or international affiliates may have done in relevant areas; state associations should draw on similar resources of their national or international association.

Some association foundations conduct research that may be relevant to an association's current needs. The association should look at information both from its own foundation and from other foundations that serve the same or similar markets or those formed with a similar mission. Many foundation-funded studies are available to the association at little or no cost if the research objectives are seen as compatible with those of the foundation itself. One example is the American Association of Retired Persons Andrus Foundation, which conducts healthcare and other studies related to older populations. Another example is the

American Society of Association Executives (ASAE) Foundation, which develops research projects that result in publications such as *Facing the Future* and *Keeping Members: The Myths and Realities.*

Many for-profit research firms conduct research that is applicable to associations. Although the actual studies may have cost thousands of dollars (if not hundreds of thousands of dollars), the research findings and study report may be available for as little as a few hundred or a few thousand dollars—an investment that may well negate the need to spend an even larger amount on new primary research of your own. Sometimes research firms organize consortiums or partnerships of several companies to fund an important study from which all the partners can benefit. These studies may be available for a fee to nonparticipants.

Government entities at all levels—national, state, and local—conduct research in wide-ranging and diverse areas. These findings may be available for a relatively low fee. One example is the National Library of Medicine, which maintains an extensive library of print and online information resources.

Key vendors, supporters, or product partners may conduct studies that could benefit your association. Don't overlook the association's members. Large members of trade associations, academic members of professional societies, and consultants often conduct highly relevant research, which they may be willing to share with their association.

Finding this research may be time consuming, but it is worthwhile. Members may be aware of some of these studies and may readily share this information with the association's researcher, perhaps even facilitating access to the research. Others in a good position to know include business partners (vendors and suppliers to your association), such as advertising agency representatives, list brokers, trade show exhibitors, and exhibit representatives.

Today's technology is also a tremendous boon in identifying what research might exist, who has it, and where it can be found. A search of commercial databases and the Internet should locate several leads and relevant research. Some associations have extensive libraries and librarians trained to search for this type of secondary information. If not, check the local public library.

Primary Research

If no relevant studies are available to meet current needs, the association should consider conducting primary research of its own. Understanding some common research terms and types of research studies should make that easier. The association needs to use the right type of research and the most appropriate methods to efficiently and effectively meet its research objectives.

There are two major types of primary research an association can conduct—qualitative and quantitative. *Qualitative studies*—including focus groups, in-depth interviewing, panels, intercepts, and listserves—help association staff identify and better understand the issues members have and the range of their perspectives on specific issues, products, programs, and services. Although these studies are valuable in identifying opinion, ideas, and issues, they do not reflect the opinions of the entire membership or customer base. However, they often are used before quantitative studies are conducted to identify appropriate options and alternatives. *Quantitative studies,* such as surveys conducted by mail, fax, or Internet, can give the association an accurate picture of the overall membership's needs, opinions, and perspectives.

Qualitative Research

Qualitative research consists of efforts and activities designed to anecdotally identify important issues, factors, needs, and opinions that are relevant to the research objectives. Effective research studies generally incorporate some elements of qualitative research to lay a strong, solid, and useful framework for the follow-up quantitative research that will—with a considerable degree of accuracy—quantify these issues, needs, and opinions by key market segments.

Garbage in, garbage out is a popular saying that is based in fact. It certainly applies to market research. If a qualitative study frames issues in the way the association's members do, if it defines potential needs in ways that the marketplace does, and if it asks questions that are relevant in the marketplace, the study will guide the association in making decisions that will improve its performance in the marketplace. If, however, volunteers or staff develop the research based only on their own perceptions, without input or feedback from members at large or from others within the association's marketplace, the findings may reflect only a partial reality. The findings will likely result in a misleading picture of what needs to be done.

The biggest mistake in association research is skipping the qualitative research—it is analogous to an association skipping a meeting site visit because it has a diagram of the hotel. Smart association executives have found that qualitative research, like the site visit, are investments that pay big dividends.

The most common types of qualitative research used by associations are focus groups, panels, in-depth one-on-one interviews, intercepts, and listserves. Over the past several years, focus groups and in-depth interviews have become the qualitative research methods most frequently used by associations.

The cost of conducting these qualitative studies varies widely—depending on the size, location, and difficulty of reaching members of the target populations to be studied; the use of external research firms and facilities to conduct the research; and the overall scope of the research project.

Focus groups. By definition, a focus group is a small group of individuals (usually 6–10) convened for a short period of time (generally about 2 hours) for a focused discussion of a single issue or several related issues. Effective focus groups don't just happen; they involve a lot of planning for location and logistics, content and discussion format, group facilitation and dynamics, and observation or recording to ensure all issues are well documented and findings are objective and unbiased. Like planning a conference, much of the work happens beforehand and is transparent to the participant. Professional focus group facilitators, who are trained to objectively identify key issues and opinions, ensure that all viewpoints are heard and keep the discussion and the results from being dominated by one or several strong individuals, can be a valuable component of this research. Using untrained individuals to facilitate discussions can result in poor-quality results, poor participation, and a wasted use of member energies and participation.

Focus groups are used to develop a strong fact base for market research focusing on myriad issues—needs of specific member segments, feedback on products or new product ideas, environmental changes that are affecting members and their needs, and levels of agreement with various advocacy issues and positions.

Many associations convene focus groups during their annual conventions or major conferences to capture meaningful feedback on the content, quality, and format of association meetings. Doing so gives them access to most segments of the membership (or its broader market). It also is convenient for members to participate. To get a balanced perspective associations should also convene similar focus groups with members who do *not* regularly attend these meetings. This ensures that member feedback incorporates all key member segments, not just those who actively participate in meetings. This ensures a balance in the feedback and, depending on the issue, may significantly affect results. For instance, focus groups with those not attending the annual meeting could help identify barriers, some of which associations can overcome, that prohibit members from attending the annual meeting.

One of the key benefits of focus groups is the brainstorming that typically occurs among participants that can trigger new and innovative ideas. As with all research, focus group discussions need to be objectively recorded and assessed and a written report of findings prepared.

The cost of focus group research varies. An association conducting a focus group in its own facilities and using a staff member facilitator with the appropriate expertise might incur direct costs of refreshments and may reimburse travel and parking costs for local participants. An association using professional focus group facilities and a highly trained, experienced research consultant would incur direct costs for the facility and the researcher, which may include travel costs for the researcher. Associations should use a highly trained, experienced facilitator to guide the discussions and compile the focus group's findings in a professional and objective manner; otherwise the association may find that its efforts have yielded few results and the dissatisfaction of members for wasting their time.

In-depth interviews. One-on-one interviewing can accomplish many of the same things as focus groups—strong qualitative support for designing surveys that will quantify opinion and perspective—but at a lower cost and with greater flexibility in being able to sample opinion from market segments that are too scattered to easily convene focus groups. It also offers the opportunity to involve members and others who are too busy to participate in a focus group. Interviews can be accomplished face to face (such as during a major association or industry event) or, more commonly, by phone.

Associations use interview research to identify member needs, assess trends occurring in the marketplace, identify factors important to non-participation or nonrenewal of membership, assess feasibility of potential new products and services, and determine the likelihood of member support for political issues and advocacy positions. In addition, many associations use in-depth interviewing to welcome new members, identify factors important to their membership decision, advise on participation opportunities, and initiate mentor relationships.

As with focus groups, interviewing involves a certain amount of planning—to select an appropriate sample of individuals for potential interview, communicate with those in the sample about the research project and how its findings will benefit them, prepare a discussion outline so that all interviewee time will be used efficiently, and schedule the interviews at convenient times for participants. In planning these interviews, keep in mind that the interview is not a survey. Interview questions are phrased broadly and should be open ended to identify and flesh out the full range of opinion and perspective.

A third-party researcher not affiliated with your association is the best person to do in-depth interviewing because interviewees will be more likely to provide frank and open feedback and perspective. When a staff member or volunteer leader conducts the interviews, the results can be considerably skewed and constructive criticism is greatly reduced. Large for-profit companies, like Proctor and Gamble, that have a staff of researchers often contract with independent outside researchers to avoid this perceived bias issue. The person conducting the research should have experience doing this.

To be most useful to the association, notes from each interview should be compiled and coded so that no individual interviewee can be recognized by association staff or leadership. The interviewer should organize feedback by the market segment it represents so that findings as a whole and for specific segments are easy to assess.

As with other types of research, costs to conduct in-depth interviews vary widely depending on the number of completed calls required; cost of the third-party researcher, if one is used; costs of the long-distance service; and the time needed to analyze the interview feedback and compile a report. In-depth interview research generally has direct costs comparable to quality focus group research.

Panels. Panels are another qualitative research technique some associations use to identify member opinion and perspective on various issues. They can help to identify and assess trends in the marketplace, identify new product ideas and test their feasibility according to a predetermined set of criteria, and act as a sounding board to test potential strategy directions for the association. These panels usually comprise members, who are selected to represent key member segments, but associations also use nonmember panels to identify customer feedback.

Panels usually are convened for a particular period of time—such as one year—with the provision that the panel will be called on periodically (e.g., quarterly) to obtain feedback on specific issues. In some cases, the Delphi technique is used, in which the association compiles the initial feedback of all panelists and then shares it with them so as to solicit their second thoughts and additional feedback based on the initial findings. Researchers use the Delphi technique frequently to assess the likelihood and timing of changes in the marketplace. In some cases, panels do not actually meet; instead, the association interviews panelists, sends them a survey to be completed, or uses electronic tools.

Recognition is generally the best motivator and reward for panel participants. Associations can recognize the special contributions of panelists through newsletter articles, certificates of recognition signed by an association officer, and brochures that summarize research findings.

Intercepts. Intercepts are random member feedback accumulated from members' interactions with the association. For example, researchers could intercept exhibit traffic to poll individuals on their opinion of an issue. Staff members at conference registration desks could ask registrants for their opinions. All individual committee members participating in a certain day's meetings could be asked for their opinions on an issue.

These efforts can be useful for getting a snapshot of member or customer opinion on an issue. In every association, issues appear that demand immediate action, and members' opinions in these matters can be helpful to decision makers.

Special care should be taken to ensure the opinions gathered are representative of the broad membership, not just the leaders or another limited segment of members. If not done properly, these can lead to inaccurate conclusions and incorrect decisions.

Listserves. Many associations now use Web site listserves to facilitate networking and to develop a sense of community within member segments or special interest groups. A listserve is a self-directed online electronic discussion among a relatively small, homogeneous group of individuals (generally with others of similar profession, membership category of an organization, or special interest) who have registered or subscribed to the listserve to participate in discussions. For example, a medical society might have listserves for its professional members who practice in a particular setting, such as in outpatient clinics or hospital pharmacies, so that they can discuss common issues of concern. Listserves can provide a wealth of information about member ideas, opinions, and perspectives on many issues—product assessment, changes in the marketplace, competitors, advocacy positions, and so forth.

In addition, some associations have set up listserves in specialized topic areas to facilitate member discussion around them or have set up listserves especially to give members the opportunity to provide feedback and opinion to the association. For example, a professional society that is faced with potential changes to the profession's educational or licensing requirements may wish to obtain extensive feedback from members and others. Setting up a special listserve or area on the Web site where members can give their ideas and opinions—while the debate is going on and the association has not yet taken a position—can be helpful to the association. At the same time, the association demonstrates to its members that it is responsive to their needs and involves them in the decision process.

Because listserves exclude members without electronic access, the association should provide alternative means for gathering input from these members to have a balanced picture of member opinions.

The following case study illustrates how qualitative research can be helpful. One trade association hired a new executive director from outside the association industry. The new CEO decided he wanted to raise the percentage of revenue from nondues income. He identified what he thought was a novel approach and called it the Country Club model.

The members were currently assessed dues based on their manufacturing production. The new CEO felt that each member should be expected to spend an additional amount equal to 20 percent of its assessed dues on association products, such as conferences and publications. If this amount was not spent at year end, members still would be responsible for that amount and billed accordingly. The board members, who represented the biggest member companies and who were most active in the association, all spent over this amount and had no problem with the CEO's proposal. However the chief operating officer, who had been with the association for over 15 years, suggested that the association test this proposal on members in three cities. These members almost unanimously said they would quit the association if this were tried. When the CEO and one other member of the board questioned the findings, they were encouraged to randomly call members. The CEO and the board made calls, then they agreed that the report was accurate, and the idea was dropped.

Quantitative Research

Associations should use quantitative research techniques when they wish to develop data that accurately reflect the needs, opinions, or perspectives of an entire population or market segment. Although written surveys are the most commonly used quantitative research technique among associations, there are several others, including phone surveys, e-mail surveys, member census, member/customer profiling, and benchmarking.

Print surveys. Researchers use print (or written) surveys to develop quantifiable data and solicit verbatim feedback from an entire population or from a representative sample of that population. Surveys require a lot of time to conduct—generally about four months. It can take up to two months to design and test a quality survey instrument, and participants need at least three weeks to respond. Data and verbatim compilation and analysis can require an additional four to six weeks. Depending on the type of report and strategy recommendations required, the researcher may need several weeks to prepare the report.

Obviously, factors such as time of year (e.g., August or December) can affect the schedule as well as busy seasons for the membership or population you wish to reach. For example, no association for accountants would think of conducting a survey during tax preparation time.

Depending on the size of the association, representative samples can be selected for populations of 1,500 to 2,000 or more. Occasionally, for political reasons, an association may want to survey its entire membership, but scientifically credible data can be derived from smaller samples if the samples have been appropriately constructed and response rates are sufficiently high.

Professional researchers use sample size charts to determine the confidence level of a survey's data. For example, for a 2,000-member association, a sample of 322 responding to a specific question would yield data with a plus or minus 5 percent confidence level; a 5,000-member association would require 357 responses to a specific question to yield the same confidence level. Sample size charts are included in most research textbooks and references, including *State of the Art Marketing Research* by A. B. Blankenship and George Edward Breen.

Designing survey instruments that produce credible, scientific data is a complex art that is best accomplished by professionals experienced in survey design and data compilation. A growing number of associations are including researchers on their staff to collect, coordinate, and disburse industry, membership, and product research.

Questions on survey instruments should be complete, unambiguous, and consistently formatted to accomplish the desired results. The researcher needs to construct the survey instrument carefully. The data developed through surveys often run hundreds of pages, including both tables of statistics (often referred to as crosstabs) and verbatim printout—both critical to determining key findings.

The association should test the survey instrument—regardless of who designed it—among a small group of volunteer members (including rank-and-file members) to ensure that the wording used is appropriate and understandable, that formatting is logical, and that all appropriate multiple-choice options are included.

Written surveys may be distributed by mail (preferably first class) or by fax. In some cases, associations may use e-mail. All surveys should be accompanied by a short, well-written cover letter—with a leader's signature—that explains the purpose of the study and its importance to both the association and the member and motivates response.

Response rates depend on the target population, the importance of the subject matter to participants, and the means used to motivate response. Typically, association surveys achieve response rates in the 15–35 percent range. Surveys of targeted groups of motivated and involved members generally have a higher response rate. For instance, a survey of an association's elected leadership generally will achieve at least a 50 percent response rate or more, depending on the issue.

A survey can be long and still get a good response rate if the topic is important or controversial or if there is some other motivation for participants to respond. For example, when a large insurance trade association conducted compensation and benefits surveys that were 12 pages long to identify industry averages, it offered participants complimentary copies of the results (nonparticipants were charged $150 for the same information). Its response rate was a respectable 46 percent. A small scientific trade association received a 76 percent response to its 12-page survey because participants were told of the direct benefits all members would receive as a result.

Respondents should be asked to return the survey directly to the association's research firm or another third party to ensure complete anonymity for respondents. This assurance alone can help improve response rates, especially if the topics covered in the survey are sensitive or political. The researcher typically will segment data according to the key demographic or participation characteristics of the sample population.

Other ways associations can improve survey response rates include imprinting the mailing envelope with copy to capture recipients' interest and motivate them to participate, mailing a duplicate survey or a reminder postcard several weeks after the survey has been mailed (including phone and/or fax numbers to request an additional copy of the survey in case it has been lost), and clearly describing the tangible and intangible benefits respondents will receive if they participate.

Once findings are available, the association should make full use of its results both internally and externally. Although many associations have developed distribution and communications mechanisms to share the results with internal staff who may need access to or have interest in the issues covered, many association executives do not discuss the value of the survey research with members. By sharing summary findings with members through a newsletter, a Web site, or other publications and meetings, the association demonstrates its commitment to member needs and encourages members to respond to the next survey.

Good survey research is not cheap, but poor-quality research can end up costing an association even more. Association leaders and managers depend on the fact base research provides for their decision making in many areas—often requiring considerable investment. For an association to scrimp unnecessarily on its research activities makes little sense.

The cost of conducting an association survey varies widely depending on several factors, including the size and scope of the survey itself (i.e., the number of issues it will cover), the size of the population to be surveyed, the cost of its distribution (by mail, fax, or phone), and the cost of the research firm (or if the association staff is conducting the research, the cost of data entry, programming, analysis, and report generation). The amount of analysis, crosstabs, and segmentation also affect cost.

Phone surveys. Occasionally, an association may need to survey or poll members or customers in such a short time that a mail or fax survey is impractical. Assuming that the target population will be accessible by phone, a phone survey is one option. Phone surveys differ from phone interviewing in regard to the nature of the questions asked.

For quantitative research of this kind, the interviewer asks closed-ended questions rather than open-ended questions that require a comprehensive response. Phone surveys are also a viable alternative when the survey sample is unlikely to complete a traditional print survey.

Although phone surveys still require time for planning, design, data entry, and analysis, only a short amount of time is needed to solicit participant responses. The survey instrument is actually a script that should be tested to ensure it provides scientifically credible data and that the participants understand the questions as the surveyor reads them. A phone survey should be tested before it is implemented to ensure the validity of the survey results.

Based on the number of phone surveyors used and the availability of members, data collection time can be reduced from the traditional five to six weeks to a week or two, and total survey time can be compressed to five or six weeks.

The cost to conduct surveys by phone is generally high, depending on the number of completed surveys required, the length and complexity of each phone call, the statistical and verbatim analysis required, and so forth. Generally, a phone survey will cost more than a written survey, given the same number of participants. The association must weigh the advantage of getting quick results through a phone survey against the costs of conducting one.

Member/customer census. Some associations conduct an occasional or regular member census. Sometimes internal politics or member public relations efforts require that a survey be sent to the entire membership rather than to only a representative sample. Occasionally, an issue will surface that is so important to the association and its membership that the association believes a canvas of each member is necessary to address it. For some small associations, it may be necessary to canvas all members to get enough responses to have statistically valid data.

Although the same techniques used to conduct print surveys apply, it is important that the census instrument (or questionnaire) be kept short to achieve the high response rate required. Repeat meetings, postcards, and other incentives may be necessary.

Member profiling. As target-marketing concepts have become prevalent in associations, member profiling has become common. Generally, the membership application form and the membership renewal form contain several demographic questions members are asked to complete annually. The form may also solicit members' areas of special interest so that the association can target communications relating to its member benefits and fee-for-service products. When associations undertake member profiling for the first time, they may use special mailings to solicit the needed information to jumpstart the process and build a database more quickly. This is an example of when a census rather than a sampling should be used. Some associations use profiling to identify the format in which members want to receive their communications (e.g., e-mail, fax, or hardcopy).

It is common for associations to compile these data periodically and review trends to help staff and volunteer leaders better understand the nature and makeup of the association membership. In addition to their use for target marketing—directing information on association activities and services to those most likely to have interest in them—these statistics also are useful for positioning the association's publications to advertisers, selling exhibit space to potential vendors, and identifying the image of the association within its broader marketplace.

The association should convey to members that their individual information will be kept confidential and will be used by the association to better understand members and their needs. The association also should tell members what other uses it will make of the individual information provided to allay potential confidentiality concerns. If the profiling information will be used for target marketing, provide individual members the opportunity to not participate in these mailings. This practice is especially important if the association rents its membership lists to its vendors or partners or to other external entities; the option to not participate in mailings can be offered on the membership application and on member renewal forms.

Benchmarking. Some associations have adopted benchmarking practices in an effort to tie strategic planning goals or staff compensation to members' ratings of how well the association is performing (or improving) in key functional areas. By definition, benchmarking is the use of certain performance indicators in areas such as governance, advocacy, information services, and education. For example, a large trade association surveys its members each year on activities and attributes of the association, such as electronic communication with members, soundness of its advocacy positions, staff responsiveness to members' needs, and whether the association provides good value for dues.

The association uses top-line survey findings—those key concepts that emerge from survey findings—for internal and external communications and positioning and to develop strategies for allocating of resources to improve problem areas. These findings are tracked and graphically compared to findings in previous years to produce a report card on member needs and the performance of association leaders and staff.

Resources

Associations should annually budget for research in much the same way they budget for other essential activities, such as computer support, supplies, and conferences. Annual budget amounts vary, depending on the size and nature of the association, the extent of its commitment to using research to build a fact base for decision support, whether special research efforts are planned for the year, and how internal or external research capabilities are to be used. Some associations require research budgets to cover such on-going expenses as member profiling.

A suggested starting point for the amount to budget for research is 1–2 percent of total annual expenses for small to mid-size associations— or at minimum enough to conduct an annual member survey. Some small associations depend on the research capacity of their members to support the association in this area.

Many large associations have staff with research expertise and experience to handle ongoing research needs. Some associations conduct industry research, including trends, salary surveys, and so forth, in addition to membership research. Generally, these functions are placed under the marketing department or in the function area that most frequently uses research. Even these associations may need to consider using external research firms occasionally, generally when issues to be researched are politically sensitive and where the credibility and objectivity of a third-party researcher is necessary.

External Research Firms

Most associations occasionally require the services of an outside professional research firm. Associations with no internal research resources of their own, may turn to a research firm to conduct a member survey when a special issue arises that requires representative member feedback. Associations that do have internal research support should consider using external research resources when issues involved are highly political or when the research to be conducted exceeds either the capacity or expertise of the internal resources.

The association should select a qualified researcher who understands the differences between associations and for-profit entities. Several research firms have association expertise and experience, and many of these are listed in ASAE's annual *Who's Who in Association Management Membership Directory and Buyer's Guide.* Another potential resource is former staff members who have research expertise and already know the association and its members.

Also, some universities conduct research projects and work on real-world projects. When working with student researchers be sure they are supervised by a faculty member, have a long lead time, and have adequate staff guidance.

Request for Proposal

One tool used by associations to select the research firm best suited to their needs is the request for proposal (RFP). Although there is no standard format for research RFPs, the following information is generally provided:

- overview of the research, its scope, and the objectives the association wishes to achieve

- tangible deliverables required, such as phone interviews and their findings, a written survey instrument, data and verbatim entry, a written report and recommendations based on survey findings, presentation of findings to staff and/or board, etc.

- time frame available to conduct the research or a deadline for receipt of final deliverables

- the process, selection criteria, and time frame the association will use to select the project vendor (selection criteria might include expertise most closely matching project needs, capacity of the firm to accomplish the work on time, references from past clients, previous projects and references from other associations, delivery time frame, project cost, etc.)

- budget available for the project (or range within which bids will be considered)

- the name of the person(s) potential vendors should contact if they have questions about the RFP (usually the point of contact throughout the project)

In addition, include information about the association and its members with the RFP to help potential vendors better understand the association and its specific needs. Most RFPs also ask research firms to include specific information in their written proposal including:

- their understanding of the project, its scope, and its deliverables

- the methodology they propose to conduct the work

- description of the firm, its areas of expertise, and background of professional staff who would work on the project

- references for similar projects conducted—past clients and contact name and phone number

- detailed description of project deliverables

- detailed time lines for project completion

- direct costs of conducting the project and how funds are payable (at times, requests are also made to identify all other costs the association might encounter during the project, such as printing, mailing, meeting logistics, and travel and related costs)

The following are tips that may prove helpful in the RFP process. Send your RFP to only the two to three research firms most suited to your specific needs so you don't waste your time or that of the con-

FIGURE 1-2

Sample Request for Proposal*

Basic information about your organization
- full organization name (and abbreviation or acronym)
- address, city, state, ZIP
- name and title of project liaison
- phone number, fax number, e-mail address, and Web address
- brief description of the organization (number and type of members, staff and budget size, core mission/objectives, etc.)

Information about your project
- project objectives (i.e., what you hope to achieve and reasons why it is needed)
- project scope (study of entire product line or a specific product or service, such as educational seminars; full environmental assessment or evaluation of one specific factor, such as technology changes; political environment; use of the Internet; etc.)
- target populations (i.e., specific member segments, full membership, former members)
- potential members, other identified constituencies (such as industry opinion leaders)
- time frame for completion (and whether there is any flexibility in this, understanding that a typical association research project generally will take 4 to 5 months, excluding major holiday and vacation commitments)
- your preferred methodology for conducting the project (or if you wish potential consultants to specify methodology that would most effectively produce the results you desire)
- description of project deliverables (i.e., components to be included in written report, presentation(s) to leadership groups, management staff, etc.)
- description of any volunteer leadership group in project oversight, conduct, etc.
- approximate or specific budget available for this project
- resources of the organization that will be available to assist in project work (i.e., previous market research, current environmental assessment and strategic plan, staff members with specific skills and/or knowledge, etc.)
- desired format for the consultants' proposal
- deadline and delivery information for receipt of written proposals

Continues next page

Information about your decision process

Identification of the decision criteria that will be used to select finalist, such as:

- responsiveness to all elements of the RFP
- demonstrated expertise and/or experience with similar projects and similar associations
- project fee and costs
- ability to deliver within project timelines
- available staff to focus on your project
- satisfaction of previous clients with the consultants services/references
- market niche/specialty area of consultant organization (i.e., associations and other membership organizations)
- quality and creativity of the approach suggested by the consultant
- background and credentials of individuals who would be responsible for all phases of project work.
- names/titles of those in your organization who will be evaluating proposals received
- date by which consultant will be selected and others who submitted a proposal will be notified of the decision.

* Developed by Washington Resource Consulting Group, Inc., Bethesda, Md.

sultants. Establish a project budget, and have the funds available before developing your RFP so that prospective consultants will know whether to design a Cadillac or a Hyundai project for you. If the association requires a ballpark estimate to establish budgets or to solicit budgetary approval, call potential consultants and be honest about your needs and expectations.

Do your homework. Identify the association's project manager for the research. Talk to other association executives or use listserves to get names of individuals and firms who have worked successfully with other associations and have the appropriate expertise and experience to meet your project's specific research objectives. Notify all firms who submit a proposal about any delays in the decision process or in the project's timetable. Notify all bidders once the decision has been made. Recognize that if the association misses a project deadline, it's unfair to insist that the researcher meet the originally scheduled project deadline.

Do not share the proposals with another vendor. It's unethical to ask for a proposal from one consultant and then share that information with another either before or after the decision is made and the process is complete.

If your research is being done internally by association staff from another department, you still may want to talk through many of the points identified in the RFP process (e.g., staff to be assigned to project, time lines). Many association executives have reported that doing so helps avoid confusion and gets many of the parameters on the table upfront.

Final Cautions and Precautions

Research findings should be used to support an association's decision process, not to supplant it. Research provides a solid fact base that—together with political considerations and other special needs of the association—should help staff and volunteers make informed decisions. Research should not be used merely to validate internally held opinions and justify decisions already made. Rather, it should be the means to keep the association in tune with its members and customers and their needs, expectations, and opinions.

This chapter presents information to help you ensure that any research you undertake will be of high quality, producing credible data on which good decisions can be made. Shortcuts to the processes, techniques, and other requirements of good research will result in flawed data and, possibly, incorrect decisions. The saying garbage in, garbage out really does apply to research.

Remember that research findings do not last forever. Member surveys need to be conducted regularly for the association to keep up with member needs, interests, expectations, and perceptions. Opinion surveys capture the mood of the moment and may not be applicable even a few months hence, especially in an industry, profession, or cause in the midst of significant environmental change. Member profiles must be updated at least once a year so that target marketing and other efforts will not fall short. But with all the caveats, do jump in. Research can be a tremendous tool for associations and benefit for their members.

RESOURCES

Blanken, Rhea, and Allen Liff. *Facing the Future.* Washington, D.C.: Foundation of the American Society of Association Executives, 1999.

Blankenship, A.B., and George Edward Breen. *State of the Art Marketing Research.* Chicago: American Management Association, 1993.

Greenbaum, Thomas L. *The Practical Handbook and Guide to Focus Group Research.* Lexington, Mass.: Lexington Books, 1988.

Sirkin, Arlene Farber, and Michael P. McDermott. *Keeping Members: CEO Strategies for 21st Century Success.* Washington, D.C.: Foundation of the American Society of Association Executives, 1995.

Arlene Farber Sirkin is president of the Washington Resource Consulting Group (WRCG), Inc., in Bethesda, Maryland. She founded WRCG in 1989 to serve trade associations, professional societies, and other membership-based organizations. WRCG partners with associations to identify and enhance member value through research, consulting, planning, and seminar and training services. Farber Sirkin is a well-known consultant and seminar presenter on membership development and retention, planning, and association marketing.

She is co-author of American Society of Association Executives' (ASAE) bestseller *Keeping Members: The Myths & Realities,* which is based on research she conducted with more than 200 associations nationwide for the ASAE Foundation. Farber Sirkin teaches in ASAE's School of Association Management, at the U.S. Chambers' Institute, and has been chair of the ASAE Marketing Section. She is an ASAE Fellow. She holds an MBA in marketing from Wharton.

Miriam T. Meister, CAE, has 24 years experience working with associations and membership organizations in marketing, market research, product development, strategic and business planning, new product and program development, membership development and retention, and communications. For the past four years, Meister has been associated with the Washington Resource Consulting Group, Inc., Bethesda, Maryland, as senior consultant responsible for market research and project management. Previous positions held include vice president for Research and Development for the National Association of Professional Insurance Agents and vice president for Research and Planning for the American Society of Health System Pharmacists. She holds a bachelor's degree from the School of Communications at Syracuse University.

CHAPTER TWO

Marketing Planning

Lauren L. Corbin and Richard P. Whelan

WHAT IS MARKETING? The American Marketing Association, New York, says it's the "process of planning and executing the conception, pricing, promotion and distribution of ideas, goods and services to create exchanges that satisfy individual and organization objectives" (*Marketing News* 1 March 1985). The *American Heritage Dictionary* (1988) says, "it's the buying and selling of goods and services." No matter how you define it, the marketing of association goods and services is a billion-dollar industry that employs millions of individuals in all sectors of the economy.

With more than 100,000 local, regional, national, and international associations, societies, and federations buying and selling memberships, sponsorships, books, seminars, conferences, exhibits, advertising space, and so forth, the association marketplace is a vital and growing segment of our national and international economy. The American Society of Association Executives (ASAE), Washington, D.C., says that 7 of 10 Americans belong to at least one association, and 4 of 10 belong to 4 or more. In fact, the top 10 U.S. associations have more than 260 million members, more than the total population of the country. It is a segment of the U.S. economy that is increasingly under competition from new associations—ASAE studies suggest at least 1,000 new associations are started each year—from existing associations, and from for-profit groups that offer products and services targeted at association members.

Most associations have competitors that include national or international associations, regional or local groups, chapters, and for-profit organizations all targeting a somewhat finite marketplace—current members, customers, and prospects. The *National Trade and Professional Association Directory* lists 100 nursing associations, 160 food associations, 61 retailing associations, 763 recreation associations, 190 agriculture associations, and 78 marketing associations, all of which, in their market segments, target like groups for members and customers. With so many people belonging to multiple associations, chances are your members, customers, and prospects are already being talked to, or targeted, by your association's competition.

The common use of mailing lists, combined with the sophisticated use of high-speed computer profiling, modeling, and segmentation, puts your members, customers, and prospects "up for grabs" for almost any entrepreneur willing to make the attempt. Given time and a moderate amount of effort, it's possible to find the names and contact information for well over 50 percent of your members and customers, even if your association's mailing list is not available on the open market.

Associations are businesses, and the sole purpose of a business, according to author Tom Peters, "is to buy and sell products and services." William Schoell and Joseph Guiltinan, in *Marketing—Contemporary Concepts and Practices,* say that "nonprofit organizations are, like profit seeking businesses, increasingly recognizing the importance of marketing to their survival and growth."

Association staff—from the receptionist to the executive director and the board—have to think like marketers if their associations are to survive and thrive. The number of associations opening customer service centers, emulating the success of L. L. Bean and Sears, is on the rise. The importance of marketing is also evident in the increase in the number of associations sending their nonmarketing staff to marketing seminars (*DM News,* March 1999).

Think about the association marketplace today. Associations that embrace the idea that they are businesses and need to aggressively market their products and services are thriving. Those that don't often are in trouble, with low or no growth in membership and revenues. In fact, recent articles in ASAE's *Association Management,* Greater Washington Society of Association Executive's *Executive Update,* and *Association Trends* highlight the growth in association mergers and acquisitions, two words that until recently were not often heard in the association marketplace. Similar to what happens in the for-profit world, weak associations are being bought, or driven out of business, by stronger, or more marketing savvy organizations.

Applying Marketing to Membership

Members are customers, and most associations depend on members for about 80 percent of all revenue: dues, nondues purchases, sponsorships, donations, and so forth. In fact, the 1998 ASAE *Operating Ratio Report* shows that, on average, the total amount of revenue individual member- ship associations are earning from classic dues sources has become stag- nant or has shrunk over the past several years. Even trade groups that have traditionally relied on the bulk of their revenues coming from dues are finding that it is becoming increasingly hard to make budget projec- tions from dues alone. This is forcing some to diversify their member- ship offerings, open new member categories, increase prices, offer new products and services, and merge with or acquire traditional competitors.

Members are not as loyal as they once were. In our grandparents' and even parents' time, association memberships were like union member- ships. If you were a lawyer, you joined the American Bar Association, if a nurse, the American Nurses Association. Today those groups, and almost any other you can name, are facing declining memberships and market share because lawyers, nurses, and others have a wide variety of associations from which to choose—and the choice not to belong to an association at all.

One major reason for this declining loyalty is the lack of time members, customers, and prospects have to devote to an association, according to Harmon O. Pritchard. This lack of brand loyalty is most prevalent among Generation X'ers—those born between 1961 and 1981—says Pritchard. Some of the largest associations, both trade and individual, have lost thousands of members and customers because of competition from smaller specialty associations and from for-profit groups and because of the lack of member and customer loyalty. The Direct Marketing Association says that on any given day the average consumer is subjected to over 25,000 marketing messages; he or she may remember 20 of those messages and act on just one.

Increasingly, consumers choose not to act at all, or don't act like they once did. On average, an individual gets more than 900 pounds of mail each year, dozens of faxes, and scores of unsolicited telemarketing calls. Out of all that clutter, why should anyone read your association's mail, visit its Web page, come to its conference, or take its telephone call?

The concept of build it and they will come is dead. The days when associations could sit back and rely on prospects to go searching for them are also fading. With the increase in competition for member attention and loyalty from both traditional and nontraditional sources, including the Web, for-profit groups, and international organizations, the need for associations to increase their marketing savvy is critical.

Your prospects, current members, and customers are more critical of your products and services, are more choosy because they have more choices outside your association, demand better customer service and more guarantees, and are more likely to leave if you have the one-size-fits-all mentality. In the early part of the twentieth century there were just a handful of pharmacy associations. The 1999 National Trade and Professional Association Directory lists over 60.

What's the best way to market membership—both new member acquisition and renewals?

1. Doing something is better than doing nothing. Don't let the process of producing an annual marketing plan take the place of marketing. Marketing must be a continuous process, and in today's marketplace, there's no rest period, no down months, and no stopping.

2. Having a written annual marketing plan is paramount. The plan should outline what you are going to do, who you will market to, what resources you will use, how much it will cost, what results you need to make the effort a success, and what you will do after the results come in—what's next.

3. Start slowly and use what works. You can always do more, but it's hard to pull back a big effort that is wrong. Learn from past successes and failures. If you've got a package, ad, Web site, telemarketing effort, and so forth that works at some level, use it. Then test new or different things against it, until you can show better results. If you are new at the job, sit on your ego. Resist the urge to get rid of your predecessor's work if it's bringing in paid results. Start from the known, and work toward the unknown.

4. Know your competition and what they are doing. If you can, become a member or customer of your competition. You'll be surprised what you can learn through marketing materials and offers you get from them.

5. Code each of your marketing efforts. Have a proven transactional database in place to track results—what your members and customers are buying and not buying, what offers they are responding to, how they pay, and so forth. Tracking results is a vital link in your on-going research. Tracking results lets you know what works and what doesn't.

6. Do not give up. If someone says no thanks to membership, you still may be able to make him or her a customer. Send recently lapsed members your product catalog and invitations to training courses and your convention. If they are still in the profession, chances are they need the products and services you offer and just may not have time to be members. Give current members and customers a chance to spend more. Send a new catalog or order form with every catalog order you fulfill. Think about multiple-year membership offers, special interest groups they can join, and so forth.

7. You can improve on success. Even small incremental changes in list segmentation, offer, price, timing, copy, or design can make big differences in the number of inquiries and paid results.

For instance, many associations can increase renewal rates simply by trying another renewal effort or by adding a telemarketing effort to the media mix. Likewise, they may be able to increase catalog sales simply by sending their frequent buyers a second copy of their catalog.

Elements of the Marketing Plan

Associations need to market their products and services now more than ever before, so your marketing plan and budget need to be a part of an association-wide, integrated plan for success.

Marketing plans come in all shapes and sizes. There are detailed ones that are several inches thick and ones that are done in outline form in just a few pages. It is not the length of the plan, but what the plan says and can accomplish that matters. Although length and format of plans differ, good plans cover in some depth the following items:

1. The near- and long-term goals of the association. What is the realistic number of new members and customers you need annually? What revenues need to be generated? These numbers need to be based on fact, past history, market conditions, and so forth.

2. Know the marketplace. Who are your members? Where do they work and live? What products do they buy? How old are they? What level of education do they have? What other associations or organizations do they belong to? What publications do they read? Increasingly, the use of marketing intelligence—demographic and psychographic information about current members and customers—has helped recruit, retain, and renew members and customers from year to year.

3. Marketing is everyone's business. Get buy-in for the plan from the top—the board and the executive office. Involve all other staff and volunteers who can help you make your goals. Everyone needs to be on board with the plan, for you to succeed.

4. What benefits, services, and products will be produced, highlighted, changed, or eliminated to attract these new or renewed members and customers? It's fine to say your association wants to increase book purchases, but if your association's catalog of books is nonexistent, or out of date, then your chances for success are nonexistent.

5. What resources—staff and volunteer time, outside vendor partners, other strategic alliances, and budget—will be needed and can be dedicated to ensure the success of the plan? Be realistic. According to the 1998 ASAE *Operating Ratio Report,* the average

association marketing staff is 1.5 people, so unless you want to work 24 hours a day, 7 days a week, make sure you take responsibility for a reasonable level of work and agree to annual marketing goals and objectives that are attainable.

6. Know the numbers. Know how to calculate results, return on investment, lifetime value, maximum acquisition costs, renewal rates, and so forth. Success or failure often can turn on one-tenth of 1 percent, so knowing the expenses and revenues are important.

7. Create a time line. What's the schedule needed to design and implement the plan and then to analyze the results? Get the planning process started earlier. If you don't get an approved plan until half-way though your fiscal year, and you're already more than 50 percent behind budget, it may be almost impossible to turn around the results before year's end.

8. How will the plan's success or failure be determined? Find out who determines success or failure and how will it be judged— by the total number of new members or customers, total number of inquiries, a 5 percent growth in renewals, by the total amount of revenue produced, by cutting overall expenses 5 percent, and so forth. You may not be able to accomplish everything in a single year. You may have to sacrifice one goal to make another.

9. What's plan B? How will you capitalize on the original plan's success or failure? Be flexible. Everything may not always turn out as planned. If your efforts are widely successful, you don't want to stop. Yet many associations simply stop their marketing efforts when they reach their desired results. That would be like Coke telling its marketing staff, "We've sold enough Coke for the day, so tell the consumers to go buy Pepsi." If things go sour, despite your best efforts, don't simply follow the plan to its conclusion—stop, regroup, and adjust or revise the plan.

Marketing plans need to be dynamic, living documents and should not be set in stone. Changing market conditions, results, and many other issues both in and out of your control as a marketer can affect the plan. Continually review and revise the marketing plan throughout the fiscal year.

Integrated Marketing Communications

Like Nike, Coca-Cola, or Pizza Hut, associations need to develop a
cohesive brand image and an integrated marketing communications plan
to promote the association. Say your association's name out loud. What
images and words come to mind? In all likelihood, the name of the
association brings to mind what your members do. If that's about all it
brings to mind, you've got some work to do.

In this MTV, remote control, information overload marketplace,
where some suggest that your marketing message may have 10 seconds
or less to capture the attention of your target market, your association
needs to develop its brand identity and its unique selling proposition.
Try this test: give yourself 60 seconds, 30 seconds, and 10 seconds. If
that was all the time you had to sell your association to a prospective
member, what would you say? What message would you want your
member or prospect to walk away with? Think of your association as a
brand. Think of it as your business. If you were in charge, what would
you want members, customers, and prospects to think about your association—that it's the biggest, the oldest, a source of the best conferences,
the best books, as the best place to find a job, network, or advance their
careers?

Many associations struggle with brand identity. Your association's
image is constantly changing and is being shaped by you, by your
competition, and by your marketplace. In *The New Rules of Marketing,*
Frederick Newell writes, "marketing is no longer a battle of products
and services—it has become a battle of perceptions of value."

Perception is reality when it comes to what your members, customers, and prospects know, or think they know, about your association.
In today's marketplace, the need to project a cohesive, association-wide
theme and message is important. Everything your association produces,
publishes, or says needs to reinforce its message, its image, and its brand.

You can accomplish this by having an annual theme and by adopting
graphic standards that have a common thread—placement of logo,
common typefaces, and color used—so anyone seeing your collateral
materials can automatically tell that it comes from you. You can develop

talking points for staff and volunteers to use in speeches, in interviews, in recruitment efforts, and in answering the phone at headquarters.

The Direct Marketing Association says its studies show that consumers need multiple exposures to a message before responding. Because your association cannot know with any degree of certainty when or how a member or prospect might choose to inquire, respond to an offer, join, or leave your association, you need to reach out numerous times, though a variety of media.

Successful marketing planning begins with a plan that knows and communicates the association's unique selling proposition, invests for long-term growth, tries new things, knows the competition, knows the numbers, prices products and services correctly, incorporates input from members and customers, makes changes before the market forces it to, targets the hottest prospects first, and embraces and uses new technologies.

RESOURCES

American Society of Association Executives. *Operating Ratio Report.* Washington, D.C.: ASAE, 1998.

Columbia Books, Inc. *National Trade and Professional Association Directory.* Washington, D.C.: Columbia Books, Inc., 1999.

Marketing News (1 March 1985).

Newell, Frederick. *The New Rules of Marketing.* New York: McGraw Hill, 1997.

Schoell, William, and Joseph Guiltinan. *Marketing—Contemporary Concepts and Practices,* 4th edition. Boston, Mass.: Allyn and Bacon, 1990.

Lauren L. Corbin has been working in the nonprofit/association sector creating and implementing new programs and creative projects in the marketing, outreach, and conference planning. She is currently the director of Membership at the National Association of Federal Credit Unions, where she just completed creating marketing materials for a two-year campaign for membership recruitment and retention. For 15 years, Corbin worked at the Close Up Foundation, a nonprofit, nonpartisan civic education organization, launching its direct mail strategy and campaign for students, teachers, and administrators. She is a member of ASAE and the Direct Marketing Association of Washington, D.C.

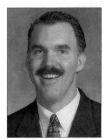

Richard P. Whelan is president of Marketing General, Inc., (MGI) a diversified marketing services agency located in Alexandria, Virginia. Whelan has 20 years of experience in marketing and advertising capacities for nonprofit organizations and for-profit corporations. Before joining MGI 12 years ago, Whelan's experience included service with a general advertising agency; he has also served as an account executive for a full-service graphics art studio and production house. Whelan is the immediate past president of the Direct Marketing Association of Washington, D.C., serves on the American Society of Association Executives' (ASAE) Membership Section Council, is a member of the Greater Washington Society of Association Executives, and is a frequent presenter at ASAE seminars and roundtables.

CHAPTER THREE

Recruitment Techniques

Lauren L. Corbin and Richard P. Whelan

THE LIFEBLOOD OF ANY association or nonprofit organization is the members, donors, sponsors, and customers who pay dues, donate money, and buy products and services. Increasingly, nonprofit organizations are being challenged by the need to bring in revenue from an ever-increasing number of individuals, often with reduced budget or staff.

This chapter presents an overview of several methods and techniques for recruiting new members and customers, for keeping those you have now, and for maximizing your returns.

Things to Consider Before You Get Started

Before you begin your recruitment efforts, there are hundreds of things to consider. What are your goals and objectives? To recruit more members or customers? To maximize revenues? To minimize expenses? Are the goals realistic? Can you possibly recruit 1,000 new members in one year, when the best you've ever done is 200 in a year? Do you have enough staff and time to achieve the goals? Will you need outside help? No matter whether your association's budget is primarily made up of dues revenue or nondues revenue, limited time, staff, and budget are almost always your biggest obstacles to success.

How much can you afford to spend on recruitment? Some associations
are prepared to spend up to the first year's dues, or total annual amount of
purchases, on acquiring a new member or customer. Some allocate a fixed
annual amount and no more. Both methods are widely used and work.

If your budget is tight, what parts of the program can you scale down
or do later? Are there other low-cost, free, or trade-out ways to reach
your target audience? Do you work with vendor partners who, in return
for mail-house, production, or telemarketing services, could receive
sponsorship at your next annual conference, free advertising in your
newsletter or magazine, or some other benefit? Be creative in your
approach to cut costs.

If you are in the middle of the budget cycle, and you are more than
halfway below your target goals for recruitment, what can you do to
ensure greater success? Everything you do should be put on paper and
shared with internal staff so everyone is aware of your expectations and
your annual marketing plan. Staff communication is critical to a successful campaign. Are your vendor partners aware of your time line? Will it
cost you additional money to execute your campaign if you do not plan
in a timely manner? Do you have to send your mailing first class, adding
considerable amounts to the overall cost, or can you use third-class or
nonprofit rates? Can you e-mail your promotion? Are there other ways
your vendors can help you cut costs? Ask your vendor or marketing
department if there are other ways to customize or produce your piece
to bring the cost down. Just because you had planned to conduct your
campaign a certain way doesn't mean you shouldn't be flexible. If you
need to take a step back and regroup, then do so.

Targeting Your Prospect Audience

Why do individuals and organizations begin or renew their membership
with your association? Why do they donate to your foundation or political action committee? Why do they buy your products and services?
You should have answers to these questions before you begin your marketing efforts.

Before you can target new prospects, you must know all you can
about your current member and customer base. Talk to your members

and customers regularly to assess their changing professional needs and wants. This is an inexpensive research method and one you can do fairly easily throughout the year. Current members and customers will tell you what you need to know to appeal to new members and customers. Have them tell you—through testimonials in writing, in telephone conversations, in focus groups at trade shows, and at chapter meetings— what real value and benefits they receive as an individual or organizational member or customer of your association. Individuals, not organizations, ultimately make decisions to join or buy, so talk to individuals.

While you are talking to them, ask for testimonials and endorsements and assess their current or potential level of involvement in the association. Long-term members usually are involved members. The more you can get members involved in your association, the more they buy into being a member or customer and, consequently, the more likely they are to renew their membership, make purchases, make donations, or serve as sponsors than those not as involved.

Also, they often are valuable resources you can use to draw others into your organization. Your members probably belong to other associations and network with nonmembers. Once you determine which members will be effective and willing to help recruit for you and which level of access they have to nonmembers, you can better target your prospect audience.

Who are the prospects you want to reach? Not every potential prospect is the same. Some will be easier to approach and more willing to join or buy; some may be too expensive or may be too time consuming to recruit. In *Marketing for Nonprofit Organizations,* Philip Kotler discusses three types of prospects: resisters, indifferents, and uniforms. Being able to recognize the attributes of these different types can help you better segment and target your prospect audiences.

Kotler says resisters are people who dislike the organization. They may disagree with the organization's principles or feel the organization doesn't do any good. If these views are unfounded and the association can refute the negative impressions through well-founded evidence, you may be able to recruit some of these individuals. But if these views are well founded, then the organization will gain little by pursuing this group.

Indifferents are prospects who don't see much benefit to joining the organization. The typical response you hear from this group is: "The dues are too high relative to the benefits I would receive," or "I can get that benefit from other associations or organizations." This group includes free riders—people who feel they can get the benefits of membership without joining. The best approach to indifference is to demonstrate that the organization's value is high in relation to the cost.

Uninforms are prospects who have little information on which to base a judgment. They are the ones who say: "I really don't know what you do," or "I have no idea of the dues, but I think they are high." The best way to approach these individuals is to send them information to increase their knowledge of your association.

Dale Paulson, in *Allegiance: Fulfilling the Promise of One-to-One Marketing for Associations,* divides this same group into nine segments: from mailboxers whose perception of the association is shaped solely from materials they receive in their mailboxes, to status seekers whose perception of the association is shaped by the status their membership or purchases give them.

Regardless of what you call these members and prospects, in almost all instances, they already have a perceived sense of the association— good, bad, or indifferent. They know what they like and what value they place on your benefits, services, and resources.

Just as your current members and customers have unique and specific wants and desires from your organization, new prospect members and customers will have a variety of views and wants before they join or buy. You need to know who's who in your target audience and approach each group somewhat differently to better ensure success.

Member-Get-a-Member Campaign

Of the many programs and campaigns you can conduct to increase your member and customer base, the member-get-a-member campaign is one of the most effective and time tested. The member-get-a-member campaign uses your organization's current members and customers to refer, or recruit, new members and customers.

Here's how it works. Each year, through direct mail, fax, or e-mail, all current members and customers are asked to refer your organization to at least one interested friend or colleague—someone in the same profession who is not currently a paid member or buying customer. There are many variations to this campaign; some organizations send their members informational brochures, application forms, and reply envelopes and ask members to encourage colleagues to complete the application and return it with their dues payment to the chapter or national office. Others ask their members for the names and contact information of prospects, then the organization's national or chapter membership departments follow up on the referrals. Many times, a premium, discount, or prize is given to referring members for their efforts.

Training and Using Volunteers in Recruitment

The first, and most important, thing to remember when using volunteers to recruit new members is that you must set clear and achievable expectations, objectives, and goals. These voluntecrs may have full-time jobs, families, and other obligations that come first. Set guidelines and time lines, and clearly communicate the responsibilities and the outcomes you hope to achieve with their help. Explain these objectives to each volunteer, whether he or she is operating as part of a team or as an individual. Explain their role in the overall strategy.

Ask for their ideas, and let them help shape both the program and outcomes. They may pick up subtle nuances you've missed. Promote volunteer buy-in by keeping your volunteers informed and asking them to help you with some of the decision-making process. Thank them, and report the results when the project is over. A simple, hand-written note or a copy of the brochure with their testimonial in it along with a thank-you letter can go a long way to securing the volunteer as an ally of your association. Promote the volunteers' cooperation to upper management, especially if they are part of a committee or board your association works with regularly.

Peer-to-peer marketing is powerful and effective, but only if your volunteers are properly trained. Give volunteers guidelines or examples of letters or testimonials that have worked in the past. Update the sample information and allow the volunteer to put his or her own personality into the presentation of information. Nothing comes off worse than a forced or phony conversation, statement, or gesture.

Using Different Venues to Recruit

The venue you use to market your recruitment campaigns determines
how you use your volunteers and how they should be trained. If you are
using direct mail, solicit the help of a volunteer who writes well or hire
a professional copywriter. If you want to use quotes, get permission to
use and to paraphrase quotes because you may need to alter the statement in later uses. If you're doing a telephone campaign, provide a script
and answers to frequently asked questions. If you are working with someone at a conference, educational seminar, or chapter meeting—whether
in a booth, behind a table, or giving a presentation together—ensure
that person is comfortable presenting before an audience and listens
carefully. Ask the volunteer whether he or she has experience doing
presentations. Plan the presentation and be prepared when addressing
prospects; it is a big mistake not to plan and be prepared before prospects.
Explain some of the goals and techniques you have used that will help
close the sale. Good listening skills in a convention booth are critical.
If you or your volunteer talks too much, you may miss out on what
prospects really want from your association or fail to learn some valuable
perspectives from nonmembers.

When making a presentation with a volunteer, you should have a
dry-run of the presentation and talk through the major points you want
to stress. Engage the audience in your presentation. An interactive discussion or presentation will have your prospects already feeling part of
the association.

No matter the venue you use, as the staff professional, you need to
be in charge. You need to provide the personal training and all materials
needed for your volunteers to succeed.

Sponsorship/Mentoring Programs

Larger members (by asset size, number of members, staff, etc.) may wish
to sponsor or pay for a year's membership dues in your association for a
member prospect. This is an effective way to introduce your organization to resisters who think your dues are too much or who think they
won't get value from their membership. It is also a way for tenured members to help recruit student members. This program gives your associa-

tion an opportunity to showcase its products and services and other member benefits.

When initiating sponsorship programs:

- Make sure that the member who sponsors the nonmember helps the nonmember to participate in your association. If nonmembers receive membership for little or no cost and are not taught how to take full advantage of member benefits, then when it is time for them to renew and pay for membership themselves, they will be reluctant to do so.

- Do not artificially inflate your membership numbers with numerous sponsorships unless you are prepared for an equally large drop in membership when renewal time occurs. If sponsored members are not taught how to get the most out of membership, by the sponsor or by association staff, then don't expect them to stay members.

- Set clear guidelines for the program. How long can a member sponsor a nonmember? How are you communicating with the non-member about who the sponsor is and what role the sponsor plays? How do you thank the sponsors? A simple thank-you letter, a certificate of appreciation, a sign listing all sponsors at your annual meeting, a ribbon on convention name tags, or a thank-you reception are some ways to thank your sponsors and make nonmembers aware of the importance of these members.

Different Recruitment Strategies for Different Audiences

Face-to-face recruiting. This strategy can be a powerful channel to recruit and retain members. This form of marketing is routinely used in trade and professional associations where the dues level is high, where a member must be approved for membership, where there is a difficult or lengthy application process, or where there are other possible obstacles to easy entry into the association. Because face-to-face marketing involves two people making decisions, don't try this method unless you or your volunteers are well versed in the association, its benefits and services, and its specific profession. Advanced planning and scripting on your part can mean the difference between success and failure.

Exhibits recruiting. Whether you are an exhibitor or a conference attendee, there are various planning guidelines you need to follow to prepare yourself and your volunteers to successfully market your association.

Meetings recruiting. What are your objectives at the meeting? Are you hosting or are you attending? How many individuals will be attending the meeting? Will any prospects be there? Will your competition be there? Throughout your day-to-day responsibilities, but specifically outside of the office environment, you are likely to attend meetings with other membership and association executives. Don't overlook these

---

Close Up Conference Attendance—Secrets of the Trade

Typical Trade Show Objectives
- lead generation
- sales
- positioning
- adjust image
- gather intelligence
- introduce new products

A trade show and conference:
- represents face-to-face contact with your customer
- represents an opportunity to meet with 20–30 participants in one day for a limited amount of time
- represents an opportunity to accelerate the sales process
- delivers qualified prospect to you in person

Trade Show Tips

Don't use your booth as a crutch. Leaning or slouching against pedestals, columns, or other parts of the exhibit tells attendees that you're tired or bored.

Don't put up an invisible wall. Don't sit with your back to approaching attendees. People will think you don't want to be bothered.

Don't wait for people to come to you. It's your responsibility to seize the opportunity, not the attendee's. Make eye contact, smile, and extend a hand in greeting. Introduce yourself. Ask an open-ended, leading question.

Don't think you can just "wing it." Without rehearsal, presenters tend to ramble, repeat themselves, and waste people's time.

Don't assume you know what your audience wants. Probe for specifics and clarify remarks before offering any quick solutions to a customer's problem. Repeat their statements to ensure that you're both going in the same direction.

Don't talk more than the customer. You talk 30 percent; they talk 70 percent. Include the customer to find out more about his or her needs.

Don't do the same demonstration every time. Keep updating your demonstration and adding new observations. Include comments from the previous customer.

venues to get your association's name and mission out there. Talk about your association and what you do. Do so positively and with enthusiasm. You never know who may be listening or whom someone knows. If prospects are attending, find out what sessions they might be attending. Some of the best networking takes place in the hallways between sessions. Have on hand some general information packets and your business card. At a minimum, get a listing or roster of attendees and follow up with letters and then telephone calls. You already have something in common with these individuals—the meeting you just attended. Personalize each letter, especially if it was a relatively small meeting and you had a chance to meet most of the participants. Make notes on the back of business cards or index cards you bring with you. Do not rely on your memory alone. Make a point of writing down positive comments as well as objections to joining your association.

When you follow up with these individuals, consider enclosing an article or reference brochure that highlights one of the subjects you talked about with that person. The more personal you can make your appeal, the greater the results. A proactive approach will make you more memorable in your prospects' minds.

Convention recruiting. When attending a convention, regionally, nationally, or internationally, you should position your association in the best light possible. You should know who the attendees are and how many to expect. Your best strategy for any convention, including your own, is *lead generation*. Collect as many names as you can to follow up with when you return. Most individuals will take literature from your booth as a courtesy, but most of the materials will end up in the trash or in a pile of other reference material in someone's office.

If you are recruiting at your own convention, give attendees the opportunity to join immediately, especially if there's a premium or considerable discount between the member and nonmember rates. When you follow up with a prospect after the meeting, personalize the letter and remind the person of your conversation at the conference. Even a hand-written note on a standard letter shows that you have taken a personal interest in and listened to what that individual had to say. Prospects are more likely to join your association if they feel they will get personalized service and special attention each time they call. If there is a breakdown of personalized service in your association, fix it before you start recruiting prospects. Do not promise more than you can deliver.

Direct mail. If you have generated specific leads from a conference or meeting or from member referrals, you know from where that list source is coming. On the other hand, if the list is of all conference attendees, an inhouse list of individuals who have been past consumers of your products or past attendees at your conferences or seminars, or a list bought from a list-broker, then you will have significantly varying results. Selecting your list is critical to ensuring a successful direct-mail campaign. Factors that most affect response rates are, in order: (1) list/audience/database—affects response rate by 1,000 percent, (2) offer—affects response by 300 percent, (3) format—affects response rate by 150 percent, and (4) copy—affects response rate by 50 percent. For some associations and from some offers, seasonality—the time of year something is sent—can also affect response rates by up to 1,000 percent.

Copy/creative package. How you package your offer for membership should be appropriate to your audience. For your direct mail piece, be creative, but don't go overboard. If you are dealing with a fairly conservative prospect base, then loud copy and bright colors may offend your prospects to the point where they won't even open the envelope. Use copy and packaging to help sell your membership.

Use the envelope. A teaser on the outside of the envelope can get recipients to open the envelope and take a peak at what the letter inside has to say. How you structure your letter, copy, and response vehicle will affect the response rate. Did you enclose a business reply envelope (BRE)? Be sure to code the BRE so you know from which list source it came. Something as simple as putting a check box on a reply card will encourage the reader to actively participate in your mailing, thus increasing your response rate. Even a small percentage of increase for your leads could dramatically affect your overall results. When you invite people to participate, you can generate more leads, thereby increasing your pool of prospects.

Features versus benefits. Your direct mail piece should sell benefits not features. Be clear about the differences between benefits and features. A feature helps to distinguish one product from another or is a characteristic of the product or service you are selling. A feature is inherent in the product—it is part of the product. A benefit ties the product feature to customers' needs. A benefit is the good the buyer gains from your product or service—or in this case, gains from membership in your association. A benefit cannot exist without a buyer.

Time line and budget. Work backward when developing your direct mail time line. Start with the final date your results must be in, then work your way back to determine when the mail house must send out your package, to set printing schedules, to schedule the follow up to leads generated from the mailing, and to determine how to best close the sale. If you are using outside vendors, as opposed to inhouse services, you probably will need to build in more time. Sometimes the money you think you are saving by using inhouse resources, may, in the long run, cause delays. Review your marketing department's production schedule. Is the department already faced with more than it can handle? Was your project originally scheduled or was it added at the last minute? If your deadlines cannot be met internally, then your best alternative is to outsource your campaign. If you outsource your package, how much additional time and expense will be incurred? Can you write some of the copy yourself or help design the package? Doing so can tighten your schedule, save on consulting fees, and allow you more time with your outside vendors. If you plan ahead, you can save money and decrease the cost per lead generated and prospect converted.

Results and evaluation. Did you do a cost-benefit analysis? How good was your list? Did you establish a benchmark or test package that pulls a consistent result and send it out compared to a new or different campaign? Are your results as anticipated? Why or why not? Did you change so many things in your direct mail package that you are not sure what triggered an increase or decrease in the response rate? Were you timely in your initial offer and follow up? Was your package memorable? Nowadays so much mail is generated that it is a challenge to get your prospect to simply open the envelope and then read what's inside.

Use and evaluate several marketing techniques at the same time. Keep track of which marketing vehicle—mail, fax, e-mail, Web site, or telephone, for example—is the most cost effective and most efficient way to reach your prospects. The vehicle used can be influenced positively or negatively by the list you use and the time of year you send information to your prospects.

Also track your conversion rate. Not only is it important to generate leads, but you must analyze which method converted those leads and produced the most members. The results of each study may indicate that one vehicle generates a lot of leads but fails to convert them to members. You may find that one method—for example, direct mail—generated a lot of leads, but in the end, most of them were only minimally interested in membership in your association. It could be that your prospects did not have enough information so that they could self-select and help you determine their level of interest. Thereby you may have received names of individuals who didn't really know about your association nor did they really intend to join. If you responded to all those leads, was that the most cost-effective use of your resources? Did it take you away from leads that were potentially hot prospects?

Telemarketing. Determine whether you have the internal resources to accomplish outbound telemarketing inhouse or whether you should hire a firm to follow up with your leads. The script you develop is critical in securing positive results and closing the deal. Invite various members of your association to work with you on the script—communicate clearly and concisely. Most individuals are reluctant to hear a sales pitch over the phone, so these calls should be used as a follow up to your letters. A well-trained staff, whether it be your association staff or an outside agency, is critical. Be as detailed as possible. Anticipate and identify as many objections as possible and develop short and effective responses to these objections. The responses should be such that they are easily relayed over the telephone to your prospect.

Keep in contact with your telemarketing team to learn of developing trends, objections to membership you may not have covered, or glitches in your system, where information hasn't been received. Staff should keep tally of calls, including time of day, day of the week, and reasons for acceptance or rejection of membership. Use this information to analyze your results. Are certain days of the week and times of the day better to reach a prospect? Should you leave a voice mail and hope that the prospect calls back? How many times will you try to contact individuals before you consider them no longer interested? You need to analyze your cost per hour of your telemarketing staff versus the overall recruitment of new members. Is this the best use of your staff's time and resources? Are they adequately informed about your association to handle general information questions in addition to commonly asked questions? Have you developed a rebuttal to overcome objections over association dues or other costs?

Use this opportunity to ask your audience a few test questions. You need to recognize who your target audience is and phrase the questions appropriately to receive the desired response. You may not always have the chance for a face-to-face interview or appointment, therefore a phone conversation, with several questions that require short answers, can help you hone your future membership marketing campaigns.

One-to-one marketing. This approach is often used during a conference—in your association's booth or at a meeting. You have a brief opportunity (about three minutes) to gauge an individual's level of interest. Make mental notes about your conversation and write them down immediately after your meeting. If the prospect is very interested and you need to send some specific information, write everything down in front of the prospect. Doing so tells the prospect that you have *heard* what he or she wants and will follow up. In addition, listening is key.

You should let your prospect speak 70 percent of the time, leaving you 30 percent for your comments. By carefully listening to your prospects, instead of trying to think about what to say next, you will be more readily able to assess their level of interest. Take a personal interest in that individual; it is that one individual who will be the decision maker so you need to appeal to his or her needs. Share personal stories or specific examples, when appropriate. This appeals to a more personal side and gives your prospects a chance to relate on their own terms. Give accurate information and use analogies when trying to reinforce intangible benefits. Talk in terms of benefits to the individual to joining your association; answer the question, "What's in it for me?" Finally, ask for the sale—the simplest of concepts, but often the most easily overlooked. Ask the prospect to join, if not at the time of the conference, then ask him or her when would be a good time to follow up—then be true to your word.

Tracking

You should be tracking and analyzing your data and information regularly. You can get a rough idea of your success or failure by dividing the total costs, including staff time, spent on the marketing effort, by the paid results of the campaign. If you don't track your leads and return on investment, how do you intend to get the money necessary to carry out future membership campaigns? Keep in mind the lifetime value (LTV) of a member or customer. To understand the power of LTV, look at the basic formula: amount of all sales to date, minus cost of benefits and services to date, minus the costs to service the member or customer, minus the marketing costs to date, times tenure equals LTV. Using this formula, you will most often find that you can afford to spend more to get and keep a member or customer than you are spending now.

You need to have accurate data that clearly identify which vehicles and methods are the most cost effective and why. Sometimes the answers aren't obvious, and that's where your telemarketing campaign can help you in your assessment. Have others in the association world look at your telemarketing script, your direct mail package, or your Web site to give you feedback.

Follow Up Is Critical

Timing is everything when it comes to follow up from any sort of inquiry. Don't wait too long to return a phone call or send out letters or other reference materials you have promised. After two days, each day you delay in returning a phone call or fulfilling a request for information can diminish your chances for success by over 50 percent. Your word is only as good as your actions. You are a representative of your association; your prospect is equating the effectiveness and value of the association based on your (or your staff's) promises. Be concise and clear in your message. Don't oversell your association in your follow-up letter or include lots of various brochures that talk about every benefit or feature you offer. Give a quick overview of "what's in it for me" and "why should I join, or buy." Give the prospect an application for membership (code the application so you can track your results) and enclose a coded business return envelope. Include a toll-free phone number so they can call you or your volunteer directly, if they need help or more information.

Offer incentives to join or buy (for example, a post-convention special rate on dues). Encourage your prospects to take action within a specified period so they won't lose interest and will make a decision quickly. Follow up your letters with telephone calls from members who might know the prospects or people from their region or part of the country. Or complete the circle with a telephone call from you. Unless you follow up, don't expect a prospect to call you back.

What should you do if you have so many leads, you can't follow up in a timely manner—within 48 to 72 hours? Put a strategy in place that uses outbound telemarketing, postcards, or additional ways to remind prospects you want their membership. Plan how you are going to package the offer—a special conference rate, half-year, half-dues—whatever the offer, make it appropriate to your audience.

Test Marketing and Segmentation

There's no secret to knowing what works and what doesn't. The market tells you what works and what doesn't every time you try something. Remember "new Coke"?

Every marketing effort you undertake should rely on two thrusts. First, what have you used in the past that worked (produced the required number of returns, amount of revenue, etc.), and what didn't? Use what works; don't reinvent the wheel. Second, once you have found a list, message, theme, offer, or format that works, test against it to improve the results.

If it's a new product or service, look at what other things you have marketed for clues on what to do. Look at what your competition is using for similar offerings; copy their successes and avoid their failures. When in doubt—do something. In marketing, even the most ill-thought-out effort usually beats doing nothing.

Test the most important things first. In order of importance they are the mailing or telemarketing list you market to, the offer you are making (e.g., free, 50% off, 2 for 1, full price, 15 for 12, etc.), and the format you are using (e.g., self-mailer, postcard, business letter, e-mail, etc.).

Test one thing at a time, so you can determine which item made a difference. Test from the known to the unknown. Test *big* things. Color and design usually are not *big* things. Lists and offers are always *big* things.

Don't be afraid to fail. Just because one thing did not work does not mean something else won't succeed. Likewise, a proven marketing effort that always has worked will one day fail—with no warning and without giving you a solid second option, unless you constantly test.

Segment your efforts and always include a test segment. People want to be treated like individuals, so marketing is increasingly becoming personalized. You need to think about your market not so much as a group, but as a group of individuals. How do they think, what kinds of words do they use in their profession, when do they buy, how much do they usually spend, or how do they like to be contacted? It sounds simple, but women and men think and respond differently, so do those new to their careers versus career veterans. Likewise, age, regional or national differences, ethnic preferences, time of year, and so forth can all have an effect on your marketing efforts. Simply put, the more you know, the better your test efforts will be, and the better the results will be.

Results

You should have clear goals in mind. Depending on the number of leads generated from a particular venue, look at past performance to gauge your best estimate of *actual conversion rates*—that is, prospects to members. Be realistic, but also factor in some risk. You can try to plan for the unexpected, but that is often difficult to do because these are invisible factors that you may have little or no control over or not even know they exist.

For cold direct mail, a 1 percent return or higher is often cited as an average industry standard. (Don't be misled by that number—response rates vary significantly based on the medium used, the list used, the product, the price, the offer, etc.) New member acquisition efforts may produce paid results well below 1 percent, while member renewal efforts may produce paid results in the 80 percent range. For conferences, exhibits, and meetings, your results may be more difficult to assess. Are you looking to increase your association's visibility? Have you attended this conference before? What have past results told you? How can you measure an intangible, such as increased visibility?

For example, in one marketing campaign, you send a preconference mailer to attendees and asked them to stop by your booth and receive a free gift. With that gift, they are obliged to listen to your pitch. To help ensure this approach is successful, be sure the gift is of value. Remember that your marketing time within a booth is limited in scope and your interaction with prospects should be different than when you are talking to a prospect over the phone or in casual conversation.

Evaluation

Before you implement any recruitment campaign, you should calculate the total cost—from the cost of obtaining that lead to the cost of converting that lead to a new member. How much can you afford to spend to recruit a new member? What is the member's possible lifetime value to the association? Are you using your association's resources effectively in recruiting new members? Typically when you use a member-get-a-member campaign, your costs are significantly lower than if you use a mailing list. Did you personalize the package? Did you *clearly state the benefit* of your offer? (This would increase your response rate.) The way you state your offer is just as important as the offer itself. For example: while "50 percent off" and "half-price" might mean the same, they can lead to two different response rates. Include all of the true costs of your offer (postage, production, packaging) when you evaluate your final results.

The more you learn about member and customer recruitment, the more you'll find you need to learn. It's an ever-moving target, and one that constantly needs to be monitored.

RESOURCES

Kotler, Philip. *Marketing for Nonprofit Organizations,* 2nd edition. New York: Prentice-Hall, 1982.

Paulson, Dale. *Allegiance: Fulfilling the Promise of One-to-One Marketing for Associations.* Washington, D.C.: American Society of Association Executives, 1988.

Lauren L. Corbin has been working in the nonprofit/association sector creating and implementing new programs and creative projects in the marketing, outreach, and conference planning. She is currently the director of Membership at the National Association of Federal Credit Unions, where she just completed creating marketing materials for a two-year campaign for membership recruitment and retention. For 15 years, Corbin worked at the Close Up Foundation, a nonprofit, nonpartisan civic education organization, launching its direct mail strategy and campaign for students, teachers, and administrators. She is a member of ASAE and the Direct Marketing Association of Washington, D.C.

Richard P. Whelan is president of Marketing General, Inc., (MGI) a diversified marketing services agency located in Alexandria, Virginia. Whelan has 20 years of experience in marketing and advertising capacities for nonprofit organizations and for-profit corporations. Before joining MGI 12 years ago, Whelan's experience included service with a general advertising agency; he has also served as an account executive for a full-service graphics art studio and production house. Whelan is the immediate past president of the Direct Marketing Association of Washington, D.C., serves on the American Society of Association Executives' (ASAE) Membership Section Council, is a member of the Greater Washington Society of Association Executives, and is a frequent presenter at ASAE seminars and roundtables.

CHAPTER FOUR

Retention Marketing

Arlene Farber Sirkin and Miriam T. Meister, CAE

SMART ASSOCIATION EXECUTIVES and volunteer leaders know that retention is important to the bottom-line success of their association. For other associations, membership retention still takes a distant second place to new member development. Yet, as any successful direct marketing or for-profit entity will attest, keeping current customers is a far more effective and efficient way to build a business than depending on developing new ones. The cost of keeping current customers happy—and loyal—is minuscule compared to the much higher cost of identifying and courting potential new ones.

So it is with associations. Keeping current members is a far more efficient and effective strategy for membership growth than is new membership development. If anything, it is an important measure of how well the association is responding to its environment and maintaining its relevance to members despite rapid environmental changes. It is the most important measure for determining if, in fact, the association is meeting member needs and satisfying members with the programs, products, and services it provides.

Membership recruitment is just the first step in the retention process. It is not an end in and of itself. Unless you are recruiting for retention, not for just one year, you are throwing money away and wasting a limited pool of prospective members. Membership retention is not the same as the membership renewal process, which is a necessary, but purely administrative, function. Research involving hundreds of associations has disproved many myths about retention that have kept many associations from realizing potential membership success.

This chapter focuses on the realities that—if understood and implemented by associations—will help associations increase retention rates dramatically and help ensure an association's growth and success. However, one fundamental membership myth must first be put to rest.

Many associations' membership activities are based on the belief that there are always new members to recruit. Although this may be true in a few industries or professions still in their early growth stages, it is not true for most associations whose roots go back more than 15 or 20 years. The early adopters have long since joined the association, as have those others who have been convinced of some measure of the association's value. Those who are left—the nonmembers—will be mainly the defectors, rejecters, and nonjoiners. These are the most difficult and most expensive prospective members an association can have.

Defectors are those who have tried membership in the association and have not found the value or benefits in it they were promised or led to expect. These may be former short-term members who were recruited during a special discounted membership campaign or promotion, who may not have been fully sold on the association at the time they joined. Or they may be former long-term members who were initially satisfied, but became less so as the environment changed and the association did not evolve accordingly. Most individuals and organizations will try membership only once.

Rejecters are nonmembers who have never joined the association. They may have rejected the association because of misperceptions, biases, or lack of understanding of its true value or because they don't see a lot of value in joining.

Nonjoiners are those who are not inclined to join *any* association and are a subset of rejecters. Generation X, those born 1961–1981, is often described as having more nonjoiners than the Baby Boom generation. Keeping the defector category small is a lot more effective than trying to recruit the rejecters and nonjoiners.

It is not impossible to bring rejecters into the fold, but it does not happen without research and special effort. For example, one large regional trade association found that new, small entrepreneurs were rejecting the idea of association membership because they perceived that the organization was dominated by and catered to large, traditional companies. With these findings in hand, the association developed a new membership category with lower dues and more services aimed at small startups. Membership growth within this important industry segment increased considerably, as did prospects for the association's future.

It is most effective for member retention efforts to focus on preventing defectors. It is important to identify reasons why others have already defected to address the most relevant factors and to identify barriers to joining.

Member Loyalty and Its Effect on Membership Growth

The concept of member loyalty is an important one for associations. An association's retention rate does not tell the full story of member loyalty because it does not fully measure the degree to which specific members (and member segments) feel attached to the association, how greatly they value particular member benefits or programs, how likely they are to be involved in any of the association's activities and initiatives, and how vulnerable they may be to nonrenewal of membership.

Member loyalty can be viewed as a ladder, with members who are extremely loyal to the association at its top (often current and past officers), those very loyal just below, and those only marginally loyal at the bottom. An association's membership retention efforts should be geared to identify member segments falling in the mid- to low-range of these loyalty categories and find ways to make the association and its services more relevant and valuable to them. If left untended, member loyalty tends to weaken over time, with those whose loyalty has slipped the farthest down the loyalty ladder the most likely candidates for defection or nonrenewal of their memberships. Market research can be a valuable tool in identifying these segments and determining the most effective ways to minimize negative trends.

Members at or near the top of the association's loyalty ladder are the most likely to talk up the association and its membership among non-members; those closest to the bottom are most likely to bad mouth the association. Unfortunately, one of the realities of membership retention is that a satisfied and loyal member may tell only a few friends but a dissatisfied member may tell many. The damage from an association's inattention to dissatisfied and unhappy members can have a broad-reaching, negative effect on its membership efforts and retention rates.

An association that pays only lip service to being responsive to members and their needs will be far more vulnerable to the membership and product marketing (competition) of other associations and for-profit entities. The stronger the association's commitment to satisfying members and gaining their loyalty, the less vulnerable it will be to current (and would-be) competitors.

Measuring Retention

Associations need to pay attention to membership retention for many reasons. One of the most important is to identify whether the association is positively progressing toward achieving its goals and accomplishing its primary mission on behalf of its members. The actual percentage of members the association retains in any one year (or other reporting period) and the percentage it loses are important baseline measures.

It is relatively simple to calculate these two measures. The retention rate is the total number of members who have renewed their membership by the end of the year (or reporting period) divided by the total number of members the association had at the beginning of the year. For example, an association, with 5,000 members that has 4,000 renew their yearly membership, has an 80 percent retention rate.

It is important that the association *not* count members who joined for the first time during the year (i.e., new members) as retained members. Including them would blur the picture of the association's success in satisfying members and disguise what is really happening. Although this may satisfy political purposes, it can disguise a high "churn" rate (or replacement of old members with new members). A measure of member satisfaction and value created in this manner is of little or no value to an association.

The attrition rate is 100 percent minus the retention rate. Thus, the attrition rate is the total number of members who did not renew their membership during the reporting period divided by the total number of association members. For the association described above, the number of nonrenewing members (the numerator) is 1,000, and the membership (the denominator) is 5,000, giving it a 20 percent attrition rate.

Associations should assess their retention and attrition rate trends over time to gauge whether their strategies and activities are working to improve member value, or if new strategies are needed to reverse negative trends.

The meaningfulness of retention ratios also can be diminished when associations offer incentives for first-year members that are not available to other members. Some individuals or company liaisons may figure out ways to work the system to their advantage—joining one year, dropping out shortly thereafter, and then rejoining to secure the incentives. This is the "yo-yo member." Churn also can occur when these incentives are offered by a national association to its state affiliates.

The retention rate often is the first indicator of possible negative trends. If negative trends are indicated, the association should analyze the data to find out why members are not renewing. The association may believe that the reason(s) have nothing to do with it and the situation can't be changed—but that is rarely the case. An association with a large number of individual members who have retired or have died needs to look at its membership base by age segment and determine how to attract younger members. Similarly, an association that is losing corporate members because of a bad economy needs to look at whether the association's scope should be broadened or the dues structure changed. The association should not be satisfied just with the numbers. It is the underlying basis for the numbers that is important. It is one thing if the numbers are down because of mergers and consolidations than if members are dropping because they are dissatisfied with your publications. Both need to be addressed, but the strategies you use are different.

Identifying and Defining the Value of Membership

One tool associations use to increase their membership and retention rates (not only for the entire organization but also for each key member segment) is to objectively identify membership value—for current members as a constant reminder of the individual and collective value they receive from their memberships, and for prospective members as a core component of their nonmember and prospect communications.

Smart association executives avoid the common mistake of defining value from only their own perspectives and perceptions of the market-place. This is an area where staff does not always know best. In addition, association leaders are often those who are successful in their field and have different needs and perspectives than the average member. As such, their perspectives may not be consistent with those of the broader marketplace. Relying only on the board or other leaders has caused some associations to make costly mistakes.

Objective research with representatives of all key segments—from active participants to checkbook members (e.g., members who pay their dues but do not participate in any other way)—is necessary to identify and define the association's value from the perspective of the marketplace. Regularly conducted member needs and satisfaction research also can help.

Once the value of membership has been researched and defined for each of the key member segments, targeted communications to members in each segment should be designed to remind them of this value. For example, the association can use its annual report to the membership to identify, define, and position this value to them. Associations also could distribute a customized report card—a compilation of all the tangible and intangible value the member has enjoyed throughout the year. For trade associations with organizational members, this should include services used by *all* staff of the organization, not just the key contact. To be most effective, the association should deliver the report card just before or concurrent with the renewal notice.

The association also needs to communicate the value of membership to prospective members and other publics important to the association. Many associations communicate these values in a general membership brochure and on their Web sites. Other audiences associations can reach with these messages include business partners (vendors), associate members, media representatives, advertisers, and exhibitors. These groups can be significant sources of new members for associations.

Retention Time Lines

An association's retention efforts should begin long before a new member is recruited. The association should know which benefits are important to that member and have an efficient member and customer service process in place. Without this foundation, an association may succeed in signing up the new member, but retention will be difficult. Once a member joins the association and finds value, benefits, or service lacking, the chance he or she (or the organization) will give the association another try later is slim.

Given the effort and expense involved in gaining new members (and, for many associations, the relatively small prospect pool), the retention effort to satisfy current members should continue throughout their membership. As with many direct marketing efforts, the full cost of attracting a new member (or customer) cannot be recouped in the first year— and for some associations not even in the second year. Thus, associations should view retention efforts—and their costs—as a long-term investment that may not be immediately profitable but will pay big dividends in years to come.

Factors Contributing to Member Retention

Identifying what members want and expect from their association and meeting those needs and expectations is the most important factor in retaining members. Both qualitative and quantitative member needs research have proven useful to associations of every size and type. Equally important is regularly assessing operating changes in the association environment.

For instance, trade associations whose industries are rapidly consolidating because of regulatory pressures, new competition, or changing consumer demand will need to fine-tune current strategies or adopt new ones to stay competitive and retain members. In recent years, environmental changes have affected most associations, with dropping retention rates sometimes being the first tangible symptom of the effect of those changes on the association.

Another key factor contributing to successful membership retention is using appropriate segmentation strategies to define the core components of the membership, identify the association's key value (or benefits) for each segment, communicate that value effectively through targeted messages, and deliver the value as advertised. Even within a fairly homogeneous membership, such as a professional society, member needs will vary based on factors such as where members work or the length of time in the profession. Each of these different groups—or segments—may have different reasons for joining and different expectations of the association that will affect retention. As association staff and leaders plan new initiatives and programs, they need to be aware of the membership segments that will benefit from them and ensure that all key segments are being served.

Several methods may be used for segmenting membership, but no single method is appropriate for every association. A comprehensive review and assessment of membership demographics, participation characteristics, and specific interests will determine the best segmentation strategies to use. One association may find the interests and needs of its members are determined in large part by their location; members in New England may have certain interests and needs that are distinctly different from members on the West Coast or those located in the Mid-West. Another association may find that members are best segmented by age or career stage. Twenty-somethings, or those just beginning their career, need basic education programs, mentors, and career assistance while those 45 to 50 years old (or older) are likely to be in a position to give back to their profession through teaching, writing, or mentoring others.

For a trade association, company size may determine member needs. Large companies may have existing internal resources to meet most of their employee needs and may look to the association primarily for its advocacy efforts and to cover the group. Smaller member firms, on the other hand, may look to the association for its group purchasing power, educational resources, and information products.

Sometimes the special interests of members will determine segmentation strategies. Examples include the type of manufacturing process used by member companies, employment settings of healthcare professionals, and the specialty practices of attorneys or accountants. Among the many ways associations use segmentation strategies to increase retention are development of special interest groups to focus specifically on the needs of the smaller group, niche publications targeted to specific segments and their unique needs, educational tracks to meet the needs of specific interest groups within the context of a larger conference, and listserves through which members with specific interests or needs can communicate with each other to create virtual communities.

Whatever segmentation strategies the association adopts, it needs to review and assess them regularly to ensure they continue to be relevant to member needs. Many associations send members feedback forms with membership renewal information to identify any changes in interests, workplace, location, and so forth. Constantly soliciting this information from members and then periodically reviewing member demographics as a whole will help ensure the association's segmentation strategies remain useful.

Role of Market Research in Retention

Regular market research is an important key to keeping members (see Chapter One). Continual research of member needs, expectations, perceptions, and opinions is an important activity on which all the association's retention efforts should be based.

Through research and development of products and services to meet identified needs, many associations have found "golden handcuffs," which create strong member loyalty and ensure member retention. Associations of small entrepreneurs have developed group insurance programs and other unique supporting services that bind members to them. Professional societies have created certification programs and peer-networking forums that give their members strong idea-sharing and problem-resolution benefits. Other associations have developed unique software or industry statistics to fill member needs.

In addition to baseline member needs and satisfaction research, several associations conduct research studies to support their communications efforts, information resource development, or other nondues products and services. Others conduct research to ensure that the association's major meetings are aligned with the changing needs of the members and the broader marketplace.

Many also conduct rejecter or defector research and exit surveys to identify reasons why members are not renewing memberships or why prospects are continually rejecting the association's membership overtures. Many associations feel that the resources they invest in these research efforts pay valuable short- and long-term dividends that might not otherwise have been realized.

Member Participation

One of the best ways to retain members is to motivate them to participate in association activities. The more a member participates or uses member benefits, the more likely that member is to retain membership. When members perceive they are getting value, they retain membership. The more benefits used by a member the closer to the association he or she will be.

Many association leaders are beginning to understand this important principle and are implementing programs and strategies to tie members more closely to the association. Successful associations are adopting and implementing motivational and other strategies to move members up the participation ladder from checkbook member to full and active leadership. The best approach is to get new members actively participating in the association within their first year of membership.

Techniques include welcome phone calls inviting the new member to a seminar or new member orientation; mentoring programs that link new members with long-time members to help them identify the best participation opportunities for their needs and circumstances; and special new-member receptions and orientations or other social events at major conferences and conventions. Vouchers or certificates for complimentary or heavily discounted registration at a seminar or program of the new members' choice will encourage them to participate and get more value from their membership—right from the start.

Making the Association Member-Friendly

The processes, tools, and media used by the association and the level of member service provided is important to members—so important that it becomes the determining factor for many members as they contemplate whether or not to renew their membership, especially where there are other associations or for-profit entities available to provide similar products and services. The ability to easily access association staff and its leaders via telephone, fax, Web site, or mail is a key component of an association's member service as is the regular positioning of contact information, availability of information when it's needed, responsiveness of staff or leaders to identified needs, and the friendly and helpful attitude displayed as member needs are addressed.

All association staff should be considered member-service representatives and offer members convenient, member-friendly service. Consumer marketing literature is filled with references to "moments of truth"; these are as important, if not more so, to associations. From the staff member who answers the incoming call, to staff on the conference registration desk, to senior staff committee liaisons—each is making a major contribution (or deduction) from the association's member-service efforts, and each contact could become instrumental in the way a member perceives his or her need for, or desire to belong to, the association. Staff should be sensitized to the need for user-friendly service and be trained to recognize opportunities and responsibilities to provide user-friendly service. Staff should be encouraged to be team members in this responsibility, breaking down the silos that can occur between and among departments in some associations.

Periodic member service audits should become part of every association's member-service efforts. Through objective, third-party review and assessment of the association's service components and processes, the association can go a long way to ensuring that it has a member-friendly interface with its most important audience—its members.

Regular staff training and use of motivational techniques to ensure their support of this vital effort can help an association develop a solid foundation for member-friendly service. Use of money-back guarantees of member satisfaction for all the association's products, services, and programs can help strengthen member perceptions of an association's service levels and responsiveness to member needs.

Equally important is the area of policy development. Member-friendly associations conduct their business openly to show members why specific policies are being adopted, the manner in which leaders are selected, and how members can provide meaningful feedback to the policy development process.

Making Volunteer Time and Energy a Win-Win

One of the most frustrating things for today's increasingly time-stressed members is to spend time and energy on association work only to feel that their contributions are not fully appreciated or, worse yet, not recognized or appreciated at all. Committee members who perceive no benefit to the association or themselves for their time and effort are prime examples of wasted volunteer resources that may never again be available to the association.

Today's hectic lifestyles require that the association make special efforts to create meaningful and creative opportunities for participation and leadership for their members. This often means splitting tasks, having co-chairs, and having more members on a committee with each doing less. More associations are creating short-term task forces with clearly defined goals and deadlines and, in some cases, sunset dates. This calls for more effort from staff and the association's officers but it is necessary to successfully motivate member participation. Volunteer opportunities should include a job description and be time defined so that members can identify in advance what their time commitment will be. Recognition rewards for volunteers in all capacities and at all levels and personal thank you's for time and efforts are all important strategies in making volunteer time and efforts a win-win for both members and the association.

Making Members Feel at Home in the Association

One of the keys to successful member retention is to make members feel a part of the association community. Once a member becomes comfortable with the association, with other members, and with convenient opportunities for involvement, his or her membership will become less vulnerable. Because new members are most at risk, great dividends accrue to high-touch (contact), high-active (participation), and high-inform (communication) strategies begun as early in the membership as possible.

High-touch initial strategies aimed at new members include welcome phone calls or personal visits by staff or volunteer leaders to say thank you for becoming a member and to verify contact information. This is also an opportunity to find out why they joined and to offer opportunities to participate or to offer mentoring assistance. This can help identify what these members hope to get from membership and could be key to retaining them. It will identify those who just want to be checkbook members— receive the information but have no or very limited participation.

Some associations use personal greeters to make contact with new members and first-time registrants at all their major meetings. Personal contact should be maintained at intervals throughout the first year. Many associations have found their retention rate so improved with use of these personal contact strategies that they have hired additional staff to assist with the process—and fully paid for the position from the increased membership revenues that resulted.

High-active strategies encourage and motivate early participation in association activities by new members who want to participate (this excludes checkbook members). The more actively engaged they become, the more likely they are to retain their memberships. One way to get new members involved is to have volunteers invite the new members to a meeting or networking event. If the new members were recruited through a member-get-a-member campaign, the member who signed up the new member would be the logical volunteer for the job. Another way to encourage participation is to promote the use of the association's products and services. Associations should consider offering new members a discount on their initial purchase(s). Whatever the means, product

CEO Strategies for Membership Retention That Work

- CEO provides a visible model to all association staff and volunteers—motivating their efforts throughout the association at all levels, focusing on the importance of members and member service.
- CEO makes understanding of members and their needs an association priority and ensures investment of association resources in developing meaningful tools to do so, including member needs and satisfaction surveys, rejecter/defector analysis, and comprehensive member databases.
- CEO motivates staff to develop and fine-tune member services based on member surveys and other databases. Target marketing of member services also uses this fact base.
- CEO ensures that all staff and volunteer leaders are fully trained in the importance of membership retention and their role(s) and responsibilities in these ongoing efforts.

Implementation Tactics

- Provide appropriate incentives to ensure staff and volunteers meet retention goals.
- Designate a visible association staff person as "point of contact" to oversee retention activities.
- Make personal contact with members regularly (phone, e-mail, or on-site visit).
- Use every program, event, or board decision as an opportunity to maximize member interaction.
- Starting with senior staff, discuss the role of each unit in the retention process, and then discuss it at the unit level.
- Keep staff focused on retention efforts by circulating monthly membership reports.
- Encourage chapter leadership involvement in the retention process; motivate them by encouraging friendly competition among chapters.
- Provide regular cross-training among staff units to get everyone familiar with all association programs and activities.
- Conduct orientation sessions for all new staff and volunteer leaders, and include an overview of all key member services and programs.
- Encourage staff field trips to member sites to ensure their understanding of member needs and the issues that are important to them.
- Encourage staff at all levels to read the association's major periodicals and to become familiar with its other new programs and services. Consider using trivia contests to help them test their knowledge and as an incentive.

Continues next page

- Focus members on the value of membership through the regular use of differential member and nonmember pricing. Keep part of the association's Web page for member-only use.

- Motivate volunteer leaders to talk up the value of membership, including its intangibles.

- Prepare customized benefit statements for all members, documenting their use of association programs and the tangible and intangible benefits they received from this. This is particularly important for trade associations where the member is not the individual, but is all staff of the member organization.

- Explain to staff the effect on the association's bottom line of membership dues and of member participation and use of member service programs. Calculate and explain lifetime income and value.

- Incorporate retention goals, strategies, and tactics in the association's strategic plan.

- Walk the talk. Visibly demonstrate your accessibility to members and responsiveness to their interests in the field.

Compiled by the Washington Resource Consulting Group, Inc.

Greg Balestrero, Chip Deale, Garis Distelhorst, Yvonne Dock, Christy Jones, Terry Fineberg, Harmon Pritchard, Terry Townsend, David Welsh, Steve Young, and others contributed to this list.

and service use equals participation, which equals more satisfied and longer-term members.

High-inform strategies used by most associations include new member communications sent within the first few weeks of membership. These kits generally include baseline information about the association and its activities, programs, products, and volunteer opportunities. They also include contact information for key staff functions and for volunteer leaders, membership cards or certificates, and reproduction logos and decals. Some also include the latest annual report on association activities and successes and print screens from the association's Web site introducing some of its key features. In some cases, however, new member kits have grown so large in size and scope that new members are overwhelmed with information. If the information kits are primarily sales and promotional materials, they run the risk of turning the member off before membership has even begun.

Some associations are putting an increasing amount of their materials on their Web sites so it is available on demand. Also, more material is being put in the members-only section to enhance the value of membership.

Packaging and Communicating the Value of Membership

Although most associations do a good job of communicating both the tangible and intangible benefits of membership in their new member solicitation materials, some forget that these important messages require periodic and constant reinforcement—to new members and to renewing members. Associations must constantly remind members of "what we've done for you recently."

Associations can effectively communicate these messages through many diverse ways and means. Many trade associations with relatively few members but high dues have customized annual report cards delivered just before or with the renewal notice listing the value of the tangible benefits used by the member firm and its staff as well as the estimated value of the intangible benefits received. These include advocacy successes and public relations and media communication efforts. Periodic, personal visits to members by staff or volunteer leaders can also be effective in communicating this value. Other media used to convey association value and achievements include newsletters, monthly magazines, Web sites, annual reports, or a "report from the president" delivered either in print form or through presentation at an annual conference or convention.

Although associations should package, position, and communicate their value *as a whole* to their entire membership, it is equally important that the specific benefits, value, and accomplishments for specific member segments be communicated in a targeted fashion. Targeted communications media may include listserves, section newsletters and programs, or direct mail to those with the appropriate demographics or section memberships. Member testimonials are powerful tools, especially when they are from opinion leaders.

Retention's Role in Association Marketing

Retention efforts should be planned well in advance, with strategies most appropriate to the association's unique market, membership, resources, and culture. The most effective planning will involve both staff and volunteers.

Retention planning should be an integral part of every association's annual membership marketing plan; strategic planning and resources should focus clearly on the association's long-term growth and success. Its goals should be challenging, yet realistic. In some cases, an association struggling with a shrinking membership will artificially inflate retention goals without providing for the market research promotion efforts or other needed resources that would be required to come close to meeting those lofty goals. In a changing environment, it is critical to reassess benefits that create value for members.

What are realistic goals for retention? The answer depends on the association's experience and the type and amount of resources available. If an association's retention rates over the past three years have been 80 percent, 78 percent, and 76 percent, it would be unreasonable to set a goal of 82 percent with everything else being equal. Chances are that even with new leadership, more creative approaches, and additional resources, this association could not stem the tide and reverse its trendline by more than 6 percent. It is more important for this association to find out why members are defecting and uncover the factors related to those defections. Core member-needs questions should be posed: Do benefits need to be reexamined in light of changing member needs? Is a segment of the membership becoming underserved?

One trade association found it was losing members because new business owners—their primary source of new members—were going out of business. Research showed that a key factor related to these business failures was inventory control. The association started a "boot camp" for new owners in this industry, reduced bankruptcies (which had also made the industry look bad), and increased member loyalty and retention—truly a win-win for the industry, members, and the association.

Sometimes it is easy to identify and eliminate the hole into which members are dropping. A California individual membership association found it was experiencing over 50 percent turnover among its international membership. Research quickly identified an easily solvable operational problem. Because of a programming glitch, the dues invoice was the only mail reaching international members. International members did not complain—they just dropped their memberships. Once the problem was identified, it was easily solved.

The marketing plan for membership retention should be completed before the association's budget cycle for the upcoming year so that planned resources are in place to ensure the plan's proper implementation and success in meeting its goals. Every plan should identify key member segments; describe market research to be conducted; describe strategies and marketing messages for effectively reaching each segment, goals for each segment, and a schedule of key retention activities, including supporting market research, staff (by department) and volunteer activities, and marketing communications.

RESOURCE

Sirkin, Arlene Farber, and Michael P. McDermott. *Keeping Members: The Myths & Realities/CEO Strategies for 21st Century Success.* Washington, D.C.: Foundation of the American Society of Association Executives, 1995.

Arlene Farber Sirkin is president of the Washington Resource Consulting Group (WRCG), Inc., in Bethesda, Maryland. She founded WRCG in 1989 to serve trade associations, professional societies, and other membership-based organizations. WRCG partners with associations to identify and enhance member value through research, consulting, planning, and seminar and training services. Farber Sirkin is a well-known consultant and seminar presenter on membership development and retention, planning, and association marketing.

She is co-author of American Society of Association Executives' (ASAE) bestseller *Keeping Members: The Myths & Realities,* which is based on research she conducted with more than 200 associations nationwide for the ASAE Foundation. Farber Sirkin teaches in ASAE's School of Association Management, at the U.S. Chambers' Institute, and has been chair of the ASAE Marketing Section. She is an ASAE Fellow. She holds an MBA in marketing from Wharton.

Miriam T. Meister, CAE, has 24 years experience working with associations and membership organizations in marketing, market research, product development, strategic and business planning, new product and program development, membership development and retention, and communications. For the past four years, Meister has been associated with the Washington Resource Consulting Group, Inc., Bethesda, Maryland, as senior consultant responsible for market research and project management. Previous positions held include vice president for Research and Development for the National Association of Professional Insurance Agents and vice president for Research and Planning for the American Society of Health System Pharmacists. She holds a bachelor's degree from the School of Communications at Syracuse University.

CHAPTER FIVE

Renewals

Millie Hurlbut and Tony Rossell

O
ONE SURE-FIRE WAY TO INCREASE dues revenue and increase the lifetime value of members for an association is by improving the renewal program. The three key steps an association can take to improve the renewal system are as follows:

1. Tracking. Determine the current retention rate and develop a tracking system so changes in the program can be assessed.
2. Analysis. Define the specific challenges facing improved renewals through research and database analysis.
3. Applications. Test changes and adaptations to the program, and implement those that the tracking system shows will generate the best return on investment for the association.

Tracking

First, an association needs to determine its current renewal rate—for each year, how many paid members have continued their membership for a subsequent year? The basic formula to calculate a membership renewal rate is the total number of paid members for a 12-month period divided by the number of continuing members for the same 12-month period.

For example, if an association has 30,000 members eligible for renewal in a given year and if 24,000 renew, then the renewal rate is 80 percent.

Note that the number of members eligible to renew is not the same as the number of renewal notices sent out. Instead, it is the total number of paid members in the association, including multi-year members (who may not receive a renewal notice this year) and life members. Not including these members in the renewal numbers artificially suppresses the renewal rate.

Renewal rates vary among associations. Generally, associations may see renewal rates between 60 percent and 95 percent. This wide variance in typical rates of membership retention is driven in part by the business model by which the association functions and economic, sociological, and environmental factors. Some common factors that influence renewal rates—both positively and negatively—are as follows:

- *Individual versus trade association membership.* Associations that offer an individual membership as opposed to a trade association with institutional or company memberships typically have lower renewal rates.

- *Consumer-paid dues versus company-reimbursed dues.* Associations that serve a market where dues are reimbursed or paid for by an employer tend to have better renewal rates than associations where dues are paid out of pocket by an individual.

- *Growing versus stable memberships.* Associations with a rapidly growing membership tend to have lower renewal rates than groups with a steady or declining membership. This is because growing associations have a larger proportion of their members in the first year of membership, and first-year members typically renew at a much lower rate than longer-term members.

- *Incentive-generated members versus full-price members.* The stronger the incentive used to get a member to join an association, the lower the renewal rate is when compared to a member who joined with no incentive.

- *Transient industry versus stable industry.* Associations that serve a highly transient market, where job turnover is high or members are moving out of the industry, tend to see lower renewal rates than associations that serve a steady marketplace. A job change for an individual association—or a merger for trade associations—raises the likelihood of a member not renewing.

Because of the effect of these business and environmental factors, there is no such thing as a good or bad renewal rate. An association may be able to do limited benchmarking of renewals against similar associations, but the purpose of calculating the renewal rate is to help an association focus on improving renewals to create a better renewal rate.

Once the retention rate is determined, the next step is to set up a tracking system to measure changes in renewal rates. The tracking system should segment and measure renewals by key variables of data that should be readily available in the database.

Key measurements vary from association to association, based on what demographics and characteristics have the biggest effect on the organization. Some basic elements to track include the following:

- renewal rate by month and year
- renewal rate by membership type (i.e., student, regular, associate, corporate, etc.)
- renewal rate for conversion (first-year members) and renewing (subsequent-year members)
- renewal rate for members who joined under a special incentive program

Renewals also can be monitored by other data points, such as the original source of the member (i.e., free convention membership or direct mail generated) or the level of dues or industry area.

Finally, renewals also should be tracked by the particular renewal notice the member used to respond. A key code or source code could be added to the renewal form and the color or look of the form could be changed from mailing to mailing. When the form is returned, this code can be added to the member's record.

Compare these data with those of previous years. If past renewal data are unavailable, begin building the history for future comparisons. Ultimately, tracking allows the association to have information available to take action and to use available marketing tools to address specific renewal challenges.

Analysis

Once a system is in place to monitor the renewal program, a wealth of information will jump off the page of each month's report. For example, it may become evident that certain membership categories have weaker or stronger renewal rates, or there may be a difference in renewal rates between new members and renewing members.

In addition to these renewal reports, specific issues and opportunities to improve the renewal rate can be identified through other forms of survey research and database analysis. A wide variety of research tools is available to gain quantitative and qualitative data related to renewals.

Focus groups or phone interviews provide qualitative information that can help the association understand the member's perspective when it comes time to renew. Some questions to ask in researching renewals are as follows:

1. What would cause you *not* to renew your membership?
2. How would you convince a colleague or friend to renew his or her membership in this association?
3. Describe the thought process or evaluation that you go through when renewal time comes.
4. Describe the administrative process you go through to pay for your membership dues at renewal time.

The qualitative information obtained should be used to influence the renewal system. For example, if focus groups highlight that members want to be able to renew memberships online, but that service is not now provided, it may be worth adding this capability to your Web site. Because qualitative information is not statistically projectable, it should not be used to make radical changes without further testing.

Survey research conducted using the mail, phone, fax, Internet, or e-mail provides quantitative or statistically projectable data to help make renewal decisions.

One technique that can be used effectively in renewal research is the fixed-sum preference scales. This technique asks members to rate member benefits by dividing 100 points (or dollars) over the current membership benefits. The results reflect what benefits members really value instead of the standard "rate these benefits on a scale of 1 to 10," which does not require a member to assign value or prioritize benefits. If one benefit is awarded a high level of points, then consider highlighting this benefit in renewal efforts. See Figure 5-1 for an example of how a fixed-sum preference scale could be structured.

FIGURE 5-1

Fixed-Sum Preference Scale Used in Renewal Research

Indicate how strongly you agree with the following statements by distributing 100 points or dollars between the statements below—award more points to the statements with which you most strongly agree. You may award as many points to each statement as desired, as long as the total number of points does not exceed 100.

I would remain (or would have remained) a member of ABC if:

100-Point Distribution

a. I felt it would give me something practical I could use on my job every month. _____

b. I had more opportunities to interact with other members. _____

c. I felt it would help me get a better job. _____

d. I felt editorial content was more relevant to my current job. _____

e. I had more time to take advantage of my member benefits. _____

f. I felt customer service was improved. _____

g. I felt ABC was having an impact on the industry. _____

h. I felt it would keep me informed about the important issues of the industry. _____

i. I felt it would give me a balanced perspective on issues in the industry. _____

j. I had a chance to pay a lower dues rate for my membership. _____

Total Points _____

Database modeling in the renewal process is used to predict who is most likely to lapse membership and then to develop renewal programs that retain these members who are most vulnerable. In one database modeling program, data on lapsed members are compared to the same data points of the entire membership. The lapsed member characteristics that are significantly different from those of the full membership are considered negative predictors of renewal. The lapsed member characteristics that are similar are considered not to be predictive. For instance, a highly influential characteristic of lapsing might receive a score of -1. A factor that does not seem to influence renewal would receive a 0. A factor that indicates likelihood to renew might receive a score of +1. These scores are added up for each individual member. The membership file is then sorted by the total scores. The end result is an array of scores attached to members, with a high score indicating someone who is likely to renew and a negative score indicating someone likely to lapse membership. When an association begins to apply the changes indicated by the research that has been conducted, high-scoring and low-scoring members will be treated differently. Members who are likely to lapse may receive additional renewal notices or phone calls. Members who are likely to renew may need fewer renewal notices. This type of database modeling is called multi-level regression analysis.

Applications

After establishing a tracking system for renewals, conducting research, and undertaking database analysis, a clear picture should emerge concerning the areas an association needs to focus on to improve renewal rates.

Renewal improvement opportunities tend to fall into three broad categories:

- improvements in promotional aspects of renewals
- improvements in the systems used for renewals
- improvements in the value provided to members

Changes in Renewal Promotions

Renewal promotions is a good place to start improvements to the renewal system if membership research generates responses such as "I did not know that product or service was available." Or if the renewal notice does not stand out from the rest of the mail, and members say, "I don't remember ever getting a renewal notice." Renewal promotions feature three key areas (1) the copy or message, (2) the graphics or format of the renewal package, and (3) the segmentation of the membership.

The copy and message. Start the new creative process for the renewal program by thinking about a theme or story line for the entire series. Ideally, the renewal series is presented as a story that unfolds with each additional notice. The copy and the signature on each renewal letter should tie into the developing story line.

For example, the first renewal notice might be a special note from the executive director thanking the member for his or her participation over the past year and offering an early bird renewal special. The second notice might be a formal letter from the president saying, "It is time to renew" and highlighting the key achievements of the association over the past year. The third notice might come from the membership manager warning of an interruption in benefits if the renewal is not sent in immediately.

Once the story line has been established, ensure that the words or copywriting used will get the member's attention. Two points need to be made: Tell the member thank you for being a member and play up the value of his or her membership.

- List what the association has done for the member over the past year.

- Include what the association intends to do for the member in the coming year.

- If the association has additional benefits and services, such as phone service, insurance, and so forth, list them. Point out how much money the member will save if he or she takes advantage of these services.

Achieving a 7 Percent Increase in Retention in 9 Months

In 1950, an association was established to speak out for military personnel on such issues as pay, healthcare, retirement, and so forth. Today, with a $15.7 million budget, it continues to speak for the soldier.

In 1984, membership was at an all-time high of 168,194. By the end of 1998, membership had fallen to 95,200—72,994 short of the peak membership. The association signed on approximately 25,000 new members a year; however, members were not renewing at a rate of 39,000 a year. Realizing that this trend could not continue, the association took several major steps and was able to reverse the trend in only nine months.

First, the association needed to tell its members on a regular basis WIIFM (What's in it for me?). A semi-annual mailing was initiated to address this question. It included the following:

- A letter, which thanked them for being a member and explained how much their membership meant to the association
- A report card, which had three sections:
  - The first section described the legislative accomplishments of the association in 1998.
  - The second described what the association was working on in 1999 legislatively.
  - The third section told them about the benefits and services offered. Members were told that by using these services, they could save $500, which would more than pay for their $33 membership dues.
- A short "How are we doing?" survey

Continues next page

Graphics and format. What a renewal series looks like can be more important than what it says. Just as the copy tells a story with each step of the renewal series, the look of the renewal packages needs to support this story.

- Make the renewal notice look like payment is expected. It should look like an official billing statement and less like a membership application.
- As the renewal series progresses, the graphics should be brighter and more attention getting.
- Test new package formats for renewals, including noncarbon-reproduction-type packages, oversized packages, and reminder postcards.

This communication helped membership retention in three ways: (1) it asked the association's members their opinion, which gave members a feeling of ownership in the association; (2) it explained in detail what members are getting for their money; and (3) the results of the survey helped the association improve its service to the membership.

The association needed to find out why its members left it in the first place. So it initiated a lapsed member mailing that went out every three months. The mailing included an exit survey, a membership application, and a letter that emphasized WIIFM. The mailing was successful, with 25 percent returning the exit surveys and 10 percent rejoining. The main reason members left was they felt they were not getting anything out of their membership. The 10 percent who rejoined responded that the mailing opened their eyes and showed them that their membership was indeed valuable.

Another change was made to the renewal process. In the past, the association regularly sent four rounds of renewal notices. The fourth renewal notice was dropped, and the other three were redesigned. Instead of a letter asking members to renew, the letter reinforced what the member received over the year for his or her money. It also pointed out what the next year would bring in terms of legislative accomplishments and new services and benefits.

These steps worked together to improve the retention rate. The number one rule is that members must be made aware that their membership has value. In other words, *tell them* of the value they derive from membership on a consistent basis.

The new look should be in keeping with the association's image. If the association has an inhouse creative department, get its input on design changes. If an outside firm will be doing the design, spend time with the designers to familiarize them with who your members are, and what the association is doing for them now and plans to do in the future. Also allow the design firm to present new ideas and concepts to provide a fresh perspective.

Membership segmentation. One of the findings that may come out of the tracking, research, and analysis done at the start of the renewal review is that all members are not the same. Therefore, it may make sense that the renewal series for special groups be adjusted to address specific concerns.

Because first- and second-year members are the most likely to drop out of the association, with first-year members making up the highest percentage of nonrenewing members, a focused renewal program for this member segment should be a priority. The renewal program for new members might start with a welcoming phone call within the first month of membership and offer new members ample opportunities to become involved with the association.

An even more specific segmentation is recommended by Dale G. Paulson, who has identified nine "precise reasons why members join and stay loyal to your association." Paulson categorizes the reasons for joining and renewing as:

- Mailboxer—someone who wants primarily a mail or computer relationship
- Relevant Participant—someone who will participate primarily through meetings
- Shaper—someone who wants to influence the association's policies
- CompShopper—someone who is sampling membership
- Cognoscenti—someone who wants to gain specialized information
- Status Conscious—someone who uses the association for his or her status
- Altruistic—someone who wants to support the goals of the association
- Doubter—someone who resists change
- Nonrelevant—someone who no longer finds the association to be relevant

Today's technology allows the use of variable copy in a renewal notice that speaks to each membership segment with a tailored message. For example, letter copy can be customized to emphasize upcoming meetings for the relevant participant and emphasize upcoming articles for the mailboxer.

Changes to the Operating System

How the renewal program is operated also should be driven by the results from tracking, research, and analysis. The operational side of renewals includes areas like how many notices are sent out, how they are sent, and what payment options are available.

Frequency. One of the simplest and most effective steps to take to improve renewals is simply to increase the frequency of notices sent. Increasing the number of notices sent to a member should be considered if tracking reveals that the final notices of the renewal program are generating a strong response. Generally, the frequency of renewal notices should be increased until the cost of generating a renewing member through the system equals or exceeds the cost of acquiring a new member. In the rare event tracking reveals that the cost of renewing a member is higher than acquiring a new member, then decreasing the number of renewal notices would be appropriate.

Media. In today's busy world, just getting your renewal effort to rise above the static of other marketing efforts can be a challenge. To gain more attention, consider sending renewals through alternative channels. Some marketing channels used for renewals include broadcast fax, telemarketing, e-mail, magazine cover wraps, and Web-page renewals.

One low-risk way to test which of these channels will be most effective is to test them on former members. If one of these tools proves particularly effective in reinstating a member who has left the organization, it is likely to also work in renewing current members.

Methods of payment. Many members do not renew simply because they do not get around to it. In fact, many associations find in the analysis stage that members lapse from *omission* rather than from *commission*. In other words, they do not make an active decision not to renew. They just do not get around to renewing.

To overcome this challenge, consider offering different methods of payment. Many organizations use conveniences like automatic credit card renewal, multiple-year memberships, life memberships, credit card payments, and postage-paid business reply envelopes with renewals.

The overlying theme of these alternative payment modes is to make the renewal process as easy for the member as possible and, in some cases, to reduce the number of chances a member has to overlook paying. The less excuses a member has, the less likely it will be that the membership will lapse.

Changes in Value Provided to Members

Associations often focus on the creative presentation of renewals and the operational aspects of renewals, but overlook the fundamental issue of value. An association that has a weak renewal series, but provides real (and increasing) value to members will see better renewal rates than an association with a state-of-the-art renewal system, but low value.

To keep value high, benefits and services should be reviewed regularly. Are the present offerings working? What percentage of the membership takes advantage of these offerings? Are they priced correctly for your membership base? Can every member take advantage of at least one benefit or service?

If the answers to these questions are no, low, no, and no, then they need to be dropped or repackaged. Every association is different, so if you choose repackaging, make sure the offerings are appealing to the membership.

Look for new offerings that will enhance the value of membership. The offerings do not have to appeal to the entire membership. An association can offer different benefits to each market segment within the membership (e.g., specialized newsletters, special interest groups, or a higher percentage of savings on the services offered).

Another option is to repackage membership benefits into bundles to appeal to certain membership segments. Test a bundle of products instead of selling each product separately.

Whatever changes are made in the renewal program, it is important to test the changes. It would be a mistake to skip the testing phase of renewals and make changes without this critical step. Testing is the bedrock of direct-response marketing and should not be ignored.

In 1923, Claude C. Hopkins, who is acknowledged as the great grandfather of direct marketing, declared: "The time has come when advertising has in some hands reached the status of a science." His fundamental marketing thesis was "We learn the principles and prove them by repeated tests. This is done through…traced returns…. We compare one way with many others, backward and forward, and record the results. When one method invariably proves best, that method becomes a fixed principle."

This same perspective should be included in the renewal systems that are developed and tested today. The science of testing starts with creating proper test structures. The key here is establishing a control package and testing against it. This is done by drawing a portion of names out of the ongoing renewal program and using them for the test. Then structure the test by holding everything else constant except the variable that is to be tested. If the test is for a special renewal discount offer, then on the test segment, use the same format as the control package and mail the test promotion to an equal ratio of those members who are eligible to renew.

Summary

Without a healthy retention rate, an association is headed for failure. In today's market, there are just not enough new members to go around to make up for the ones that leave. To keep existing members, an association must do the following:

- Determine its present retention rate.

- Analyze why members are leaving, using exit surveys, and act accordingly on the information accumulated.

- Actively pursue lapsed members.

- Evaluate the look of the renewal package and change it if necessary.

- Evaluate the frequency of the renewal mailings, and adjust it if necessary.

Most important, an association must show members that their membership does have value—in other words, "What's in it for me?"

RESOURCES

Hopkins, Claude C. *Scientific Advertising.* Lincolnwood, Ill.: NTC Business Books, 1991.

Levin, Mark. *Membership Development: 101 Ways to Get and Keep Your Members!* Columbia, Md.: BAI, Inc., 1997.

Paulson, Dale G. *Allegiance: Fulfilling the Promise of One-to-One Marketing for Associations.* Washington, D.C.: American Society of Association Executives, 1998.

Millie Hurlbut is director of marketing for the Association of the United States Army (AUSA). Before joining AUSA, Hurlbut served as director of development for the Society of Independent Gasoline Marketers of America, a trade association in Reston, Virginia.

Hurlbut has also served as president of Women in Advertising & Marketing, Washington, D.C. She presently serves on the Membership Section Council of the American Society of Association Executives and the Membership Advisory Council of the Greater Washington Society of Association Executives.

Tony Rossell is senior vice president for Marketing General Inc., (MGI), a diversified marketing services company located in Alexandria, Virginia. Rossell has been with MGI since 1985 and has 17 years of marketing experience working almost exclusively with associations and education organizations.

Rossell has written extensively on marketing for educational and nonprofit organizations. His articles have appeared in *Association Trends, School Marketing Newsletter,* and the American Marketing Association's *Insight.*

CHAPTER SIX

Developing Materials

Jamie Lee DeSimone

THEORETICALLY, AN ASSOCIATION'S image, logo, and collateral materials should coordinate like a well-decorated home. In an ideal world, all the pieces would match, the feel would be consistent, and the prospect or buyer would be enticed. Generally, a decorator wouldn't mix a colonial-style plaid couch with a post-modern steel-and-glass coffee table, so why should you send mixed collateral materials to prospective new members? Before embarking on any design project, consider multiple factors, including image, style, and branding, to ensure the unity of the design and message in all the various forms of membership marketing materials you present.

Using Your Marketing Plan

In a nutshell, the purpose of an association is to serve its membership. Therefore, the purpose of a membership marketing professional is to act as a member advocate, by promoting the features and benefits of membership that are most beneficial to the prospective member. The development of any membership marketing plan, as discussed in Chapter 2, should include the framework for creating association-wide employee buy in and a customer-oriented culture, if one doesn't already exist.

When the plan is ready to implement, you, as a part of the membership team, will be key to disseminating information throughout the association concerning any changes in image, style and graphic standards, branding, taglines, and logo.

Recognizing and Reinforcing Your Association's Image Through Style

In this chapter, style is defined as tangible, visual nuances that are specific to your organization. For example, in its documents, the National Association of Independent Schools does not capitalize position titles. The title is capitalized only when it is used in a proper address or on a name badge. This is done primarily for effect; there is no statement being made.

Image, on the other hand, is defined as less tangible, emotionally centered feelings toward an association or product generated by marketing and advertising. For example, the Hallmark greeting card company makes you think sentiment, which is what its advertising campaigns focus on. It sponsors sentimental movies on network television and has commercials in which people become emotional after receiving one of its greeting cards. Consumers look for the Hallmark logo on the back of a card. It doesn't mean that another greeting card company doesn't make equally sentimental cards, but Hallmark's advertisements emit warm, fuzzy feelings.

Although image and style can be separated by definition, they work in tandem to define the look and feel of your association. In *Do-It-Yourself Direct Marketing,* Mark Bacon states that "by using the same company logo, similar design principles, and even the same typeface for ads, the company establishes an image and reinforces it at every opportunity." Using a unified visual image is one of the best ways for associations to gain universal recognition.

Many small associations choose to hire an outside designer to design a logo or trademark. Even associations with inhouse designers may choose to go to an outside designer for a fresh idea. A logo should be representative of your constituency. For example, a medical association may want its logo to have an element that is reflective of the medical profession, such as a stethoscope. The logo you select should enhance your association's image, increase awareness of the work performed by your constituency, be up to date, reinforce brand recognition, and create a visual effect that will remind the public of the field your association represents.

Style and Graphic Standards

To ensure continuity, all businesses should develop and adhere to a style guide. A style guide establishes standards for consistency to help maintain the image and identity of the organization. It should be both specific enough to be clear about results and flexible. It should identify the preferred fonts, logo-specific colors, and distinct guidelines that keep grammar and language consistent. The look of an association tends to change with its staff; a style guide helps to prevent that from happening.

In addition to a style guide, all businesses should have a list of graphics that may be used in promotions. Graphic standards help to maintain an established look, and help consumers identify who the product is from and, in some cases, what it is. A good design incorporates graphics and text and uses white space effectively.

Projecting Your Image

Barron's *Dictionary of Marketing Terms* defines image as "1. Visual counterpart or likeness of an object, a person, or a scene produced by an optical device such as a mirror or camera. 2. Illusory conception created by advertising and projected by the media, that embodies emotions, perceptions, attitudes, and intellectual orientation of a group toward an entity." What image should your association project? What image would your potential members be drawn to?

What do you want to be to whom? In some cases, a long-range strategic plan will help you and your board decide whom your organization wants to serve, what services and benefits you want to provide to your members, and what you want to accomplish in the future. An organization that attempts to be everything to everyone often ends up being nothing to anyone. You know what your association does and provides, but what image do you want to project? Do you want to be thought of as a group that gives its seal of approval to members? Do you

want to be thought of as a resource group that holds all the answers?
Are you primarily a legislative organization?

Branding and Being Aware of the Competition

Who are your competitors and where does your association fall within
the competition? Barron's *Dictionary of Marketing Terms* defines positioning as a "marketing strategy that attempts to control the perception of a
product or service relative to competitive products or services." Positioning needs to be reevaluated regularly because it depends on the current
market for a specific product or service.

You should develop a positioning statement, and stick to it. Here is a
sample format suggested by Tim Ambler in *Marketing From Advertising to
Zen:*

• Brand description. This should be a paragraph that includes your
  mission statement and products and services.

• Consumer proposition. This should be a short, strategic statement,
  possibly the tagline that distinguishes you to your target audience.

• Target member. This should outline the type of members you are
  trying to attract, as well as possible nonmember consumers for
  products or services offered by the association.

• Target competitor. Although most associations have a niche, almost
  everyone has some form of competition. The competitor may not
  be a full-service association, but some other competitor that offers
  similar benefits and services. Learn who your competitors are, and
  list them.

• Differentiation. This is how your association or specific products
  and services differ from your competitors.

• Preference. Why are you better?

• Pricing strategy. What are the different pricing levels offered for
  membership, products, and services? How do they compare on an
  a la carte level? How does the total pricing compare with your
  competitors?

- Target channel. Which member group (if you have more than one) matters most?

- Trade factors. Apart from the above factors, why does your association's specific field of focus require or need an association?

Branding, on the other hand, means that whatever the product or service is, it carries a preconception of the quality or guarantee that stands behind it. Everyone has seen car advertisements on television. When the Mercedes-Benz logo appears, what comes to mind? Quality. How about Volvo? Safety. How about Saturn? Haggle-free pricing. What comes to mind when someone sees your association logo? In the case of the American Automobile Association (AAA), the AAA sticker on a tow truck projects an image of safety; on a hotel sign, it projects quality and cleanliness. Branding works by allowing associations to decide how they choose to be perceived by the public.

Logos and Taglines

AAA has strong logo recognition. Who doesn't recognize the three red capital A's with an oval-shaped swish around them? With the thousands of associations in existence, not everyone can expect the same logo recognition, but do target members recognize the logo? Not every person walking down the street may recognize the lower case nea logo of the National Education Association, but you can bet that almost all U.S. teachers do. Does your target audience recognize your logo?

When developing a new logo, consider the following:

- The logo should work as well in color (your specific association colors) as it does in black and white. Many businesses choose elaborate logos that don't translate well into a simple black-and-white document.

- The logo should contain the whole association name. Many associations choose to develop a long and short version of a logo: one that is a graphic only, and one that contains the graphic and the name. Depending on the use, do not assume the member knows who sent the materials.

• Use a graphic image, if possible. Your image can be a word or picture. If it is a word, set it apart from other text by using a special font that is used only for your logo. You can also set apart text logos with color. Graphic images are easy to work with and don't clutter text. The logo should be developed in a tagged image file (.tif) format, which is an uncompressed image that offers the highest quality reproduction. It offers a true interpretation of an image and should be used by an inhouse or outside designer to insert the logo into all document types. Because the .tif format is uncompressed, it takes up a lot of disk space, so you should also have the logo developed in a PostScript document file (.pdf) format, which is more portable and suitable for e-mailing or using on a Web site. This type of image is static and is best used for preserving both text and image in documents such as online membership applications. The .pdf format allows for a print-out of an exact document.

• Design a logo that will withstand excessive use. You will and should use your logo on every item that leaves the association.

• Don't expect to change the logo without having a marketing plan and branding campaign to support the change. When the Center for Healthcare Information Management in Ann Arbor, Mich., decided to design a new logo, it went a step further and created a new corporate communications plan. This plan detailed all communications, including industry awareness, program promotion, business letters, and e-mails. One of the key functions of the transition was keeping staff informed, asking for input, and creating buy-in to keep the passage smooth. It created a new branding campaign and revamped its marketing plan to include the organization's new vision, new programs, diversification of membership, and a demonstration of commitment to its industry.

• Follow the logo with a tagline or catch phrase. "Just do it," the slogan of the Nike generation, conjures an image of athletes, challenges, and, oh yeah, the sales of sports equipment bearing the famous swoosh symbol. "Got milk?" is the slogan used by the National Fluid Milk Processor Promotion Board. The board itself might not be recognized as a national entity, but every time a white-mustache-laden celebrity appears with his or her milky grin, it makes you want to reach for the carton in your refrigerator. Taglines can be very effective if they are kept succinct, descriptive, and properly placed in the marketing materials.

Identifying Your Resources

Because most associations have budgets, don't try to reinvent the wheel. To get the greatest member response for the least investment, inventory the items already available. Review materials that already exist and how they fit with the marketing plan. In some cases, there may already be an effective set of membership marketing pieces, but the way in which they are used must be improved. In other cases, looking at what already exists may make one wonder how the organization ever attracted a member in the first place.

The following is a list of items that already exist in most associations that you can draw on for ideas and information to use in new marketing pieces:

- articles and newsletters
- brochures
- flyers
- old conference programs
- publications lists
- postcards announcing new products or services
- a Web site
- press releases
- information or fact sheets
- published newspaper articles
- letters from members

In most cases, the effective tools for attracting new members already exist. The key is to repackage them in a way that they will complement each other and work together to improve membership and retention.

Improving on What You Already Have

Review the promotional materials you have. Anything you send out of
your office is promotional material. Take your business card, for instance.
Does it have the association name, address, phone number, fax number,
e-mail address, and Web site address? Does it have your name and title?
What else does it have? What's on the back? Mission statement? Highlight of products and services? Don't waste that space on the back of
your business card—use it. It doesn't cost much more to print the back-
side of a business card, and with just a few words, you could make a
statement.

Use a membership footer on all resource-type documents that leave
your office. If someone shares that document with a nonmember, that
nonmember may be impressed with the information and want to join.
The information on how to join is right there.

In addition to maintaining continuity in style and graphic standards,
you also need to ensure the same message is being told. Most associations take stands on certain issues that affect the membership majority.
Communicate those positions throughout the association and especially
to everyone in the membership and marketing departments. Generally,
membership is the first line of contact for nonmembers, so be sure you
are communicating the proper message.

Associations use hundreds of materials. The most important thing to
include in any promotional material is contact information containing
not just addresses and phone numbers, but fax numbers, Web site
addresses, e-mail addresses, and the complete association name with
logo. Every item that leaves the association should contain the association's logo—no exceptions. Promotional materials should also include
the following:

- Advertisements. Include the association's name and complete contact
  information; assume your association is not well known and that you
  always need to identify it. Always include your logo.

- Annual reports. Include photos of employees; make your association
  "real" to your membership. Include a sidebar of new products or
  services.

- Brochures. Address customer benefits. Tell how membership in your organization will help your prospect's bottom line. Keep information about benefits short and to the point; allow room for graphics and white space. Include photos and testimonials. Consider this the only chance for your association to make a first impression. What do you want that impression to be? Exclude names of employees that are subject to change. Don't include information that will quickly make the document obsolete.

- Business cards. Besides the typical information on the front, use the back; include the mission or some other statement about the work of the association

- Calendars. List all events and describe them. Include membership information.

- Conference and workshop brochures. Include membership information on every brochure promoting an association event or service. Chances are these brochures will fall into the hands of nonmembers, and you want to make it as easy as possible for them to join.

- E-mail signatures. Include name, title, association name and/or logo, contact information, and Web site information. Add a tagline or mission statement if possible.

- Envelopes. Include the logo, association name, and return address. If the envelope will hold information that has been requested, add wording to the envelope indicating "membership information enclosed." People will be looking out for it. If it is a direct-mail piece, use a teaser, but don't trick the audience with sweepstakes-style information. Sly wording and phony "express mail" envelopes can annoy some people.

- Fax cover sheets. Include upcoming conference dates and complete contact information. Don't let dead space go to waste—mention your membership slogan or special promotions, such as member-get-a-member campaigns.

- Invoices. Include contact information and logo.

- Inserts. Use in association magazines or journals to promote subscriptions or encourage membership information requests.

- Joined member kits. Create an outline or "snapshot" of member benefits. Include a "call list" of departments and services offered. Design a folder-type document with pages and inserts that can be brought up to date and kept current with upcoming conferences and events. Keep them short, to the point, and easy to reference. Design a piece that can be kept handy—perhaps a folder with a file tab for easy access.

- Journals and magazines. Make the most of the generally wide distribution of these items. Include a page about your association, subscription information, and membership information. Although it's important to leave valuable advertising space available, do not bury your contact information in the middle of the magazine. Magazines generally are shared with nonmembers and can be effective promotional pieces to give out at conferences and other networking events. If budget allows, include a subscription or membership (or both) reply card in the magazine. Your magazine should have a recognizable style that is easily identified by the readers.

- Letterhead. Ensure all letterhead contain contact information and the logo. Include the association's Web site address.

- Membership applications. Include contact information people can use when they have questions. The application may get separated from the rest of the information, so make it easy to identify.

- Membership cards. Include logo and contact information. Include expiration date to aid in the renewal process.

- Newsletters. Include contact, subscription, and membership information.

- Postcard invites for more information. Use as a call-to-action piece. This may be appropriate for associations with expensive and overwhelming membership applications or procedures. It helps to attract interest before prospects are deterred by the application process.

Smaller budget associations that usually send a "prospective member package" should send a short brochure with postcard reply instead.

• Prospective member package. Use in associations with a complex and extensive membership process. Packages should include an outline of the membership process and when the applicant may expect a response. Include complete information referring to fees, certification or accreditation requirements (and where to get them if they are not provided by the association), relevant background information, and a list of benefits and services the member may receive if accepted.

• Publication lists. Include these in every publication sold. Also include membership information in book orders going to nonmembers.

• Stickers and decals. Should be recognizable and contain the logo and complete name of the association.

• White papers. Include logo and association name on every page. These items get photocopied and passed around (even if the reader doesn't obtain permission).

Testimonials

Sometimes the testimonial of a well-known or respected colleague will prompt a prospective member to join. By using a testimonial, you communicate to prospects that they are not alone and that others value the products and services your organization provides. When using testimonials, consider using a recognized name and a photo. If your membership is such that there is no recognizable name, using a picture adds identity to the person and makes it more "real" to the reader. Photos should be taken in the person's work place to make him or her visually identifiable to the potential member. When using testimonials, keep it in the person's language, don't overpolish the statement, get permission and give full attribution, and group testimonials together in your marketing piece for the most impact.

Direct Mail with First-Class Appeal

Because direct mail is the most common form of association membership solicitation, direct mail pieces need to be imaginative, informative, and effective. The ability to target potential member segments and personalize your letter or direct mail piece makes this type of solicitation cost effective and essential to a good membership drive. Each piece should include a response device, such as an application or reply card.

How effective is your particular piece? When developing your direct mail plan, gauge the effectiveness of each piece by using a simple coding system that allows you to track how a prospect found out about your association. For example, a direct mail campaign targeting different prospect groups may be coded according to where the name came from (e.g., nonmember subscribers, nonmember conference attendees) and when it was sent (e.g., 6/99). At the end of the year, this tracking system will help you gauge the effectiveness of the campaign and each of the pieces used. This simple tracking system can help you focus on the effective mail efforts and help to improve the ineffective ones.

Creating New Marketing Pieces

As with all service organizations, there comes a time when the membership must be polled for its opinion. It is pointless to continue using brochures, postcards, and direct mail pieces that have shown to be ineffective for recruiting new members. For the purposes of membership marketing only, ask the following questions, not of your audience, but of your membership team before you embark on new ventures:

- What is considered a good response? (This question should be asked and answered in the original marketing plan.)
- Are you communicating your message?
- Have you attracted new members?
- Does the product or service address the need as originally identified?
- If not, is it the need that should be reevaluated, or the product or service?
- Are you being cost effective?

In the field of fund-raising, it is better to focus your time and attention on 10 people who are able to donate $100,000 a piece to your cause than to approach 1,000 people who are able to give only $100 apiece. Apply that same rule to marketing for prospective members. If you have the resources, create a more costly marketing piece by producing fewer pieces and targeting your best prospective member pool. In your secondary marketing effort, send a less-expensive piece to a broader audience. In the long run, this approach will cost less and yield a larger return.

Get the Most from Your Budget

Deciding what you can afford to do, what fits your image, and what will be most effective for the cost is one of the greatest challenges in developing membership marketing materials. There are four basic design decisions to be made for every printed piece:

1. paper grade (grade is determined by weight, in pounds, and coated vs. uncoated)
2. number of colors required (1-, 2-, or 4-color ink, or 4-color process)
3. number of paper folds
4. paper size

Consult with a printer or designer to help you decide how to combine products to achieve the best-looking marketing piece for your budget. Four-color projects are typically more costly and look expensive, so if the membership has been vocal about dues increases, this would not be an appropriate choice. If you have a small budget, using high-quality paper with two-color ink is generally a good way to start. Four-color and four-color process have become less costly over the past few years. You may be able to do a four-color piece for nearly the same money as a two-color piece, especially if you are doing a large print run. Many printers located outside metropolitan areas can afford to keep their costs low. If you have the time, it may be cost effective to send your documents out of state to be printed.

Associations operating on a shoestring budget should be careful that their major marketing materials will not quickly become out of date. Create pieces that, while informative and enticing, are not filled with date-sensitive materials, such as dates of conference and workshop dates and names of specific employees. Associations should have separate e-mail addresses for their membership office and any other office that is advertised in their publications to keep it generic. (For example, instead of listing your membership contact as johndoe@association.org, list it as membership@association.org.)

Inexpensive collateral pieces can be created using coordinated papers, envelopes, and cards from a paper supply company or office supply store. These can be produced directly from your laser printer. As with all printing, check the costs involved to ensure this is the most cost-effective way to produce the piece.

Associations with large budgets have the opportunity to be creative. Develop a marketing piece that illustrates the type of work you do. If you represent a nursing association, send out an invitation to join on a large adhesive strip or tongue depressor. Keep ideas fresh and redo marketing pieces as often as time and budget allow. What fails to attract a prospect one year may succeed the next year in a new design.

Should You Use a Designer?

Working with an outside designer is nearly as hands on as if you were doing the work inhouse. Make sure you select a designer based on a portfolio and not just a recommendation. Whom someone may recommend to you may not be the person reflective of your association's style. Once you've picked a designer, give him or her samples of materials you have. Good designers spend a lot of time educating themselves about your organization so that they can do the best job for you. Then, sit down with the designer and explain to him or her your target audience and what you expect from the piece he or she is about to design, then listen to some of the ideas the designer already may have. Share any ideas you have. Keep the lines of communication open throughout the process. Most important, don't be afraid to say no, or request changes— you don't have to like it just because an expert is designing it. Make sure you proof the document every step of the way, and if you have the time, give the piece to friends who don't know much about your association. Ask them to look it over and see if it answers any questions they would have about joining your organization. Ask them what their impression is of the piece.

Reasons to choose investing in an outside designer may include the following:

1. You need to invest in membership efforts. The old saying "you have to spend money to make money" rings true when it comes to increasing association membership.
2. You need to differentiate your organization from other organizations by using splashier, more creative marketing pieces.
3. You need to highlight a new membership level or effort that you want to have stand out from your other membership levels.
4. You need to incorporate new logos, slogans, and themes into one new package worthy of a global unveiling.
5. You need to streamline or simplify marketing pieces that are out of date.

The following are things to consider before deciding to use an outside designer:

1. Is it affordable? Designers aren't inexpensive, but you generally can reduce your costs with a particular designer if you agree to let him or her do a whole series of pieces for you.
2. Is the association getting the most for its money? If you are going to hire a designer, then let them design something. All too often, people have designers design a simple piece that could have been designed inhouse.
3. Do you have the time to work with an outside designer? Sending something outside to be developed may save time, but to save a lot of anguish, you must remain in control of the product.
4. Do not be afraid to say no to a designer. The designer is being paid to provide a service, if it does not meet the standards of the association, make a change.
5. Can the designer also provide editorial services? You will be able to take some of the pressure off of yourself by enabling the designer to edit or enhance your copy while designing the piece.

Keep the following in mind when choosing a designer:

- Define the objectives of the marketing pieces to be designed.
- Assemble the names of desirable designers with the appropriate credentials.
- Contact the most desirable designers.
- Choose a group of finalists to be interviewed.
- View portfolios and check references.
- Evaluate the level of trust and comfort you have with them.
- Discuss details of the cost of the project—draw up appropriate contracts.
- Thoroughly inform the designer about your association.
- Consider the advantages of staying with one designer—price for multiple pieces, know how you work, shorter turnaround time, and so forth.

Alternative Membership Marketing Means

Contrary to popular belief, not all members are recruited via mail or phone. Face-to-face contact always will be an effective recruitment technique, and exhibit booths play a key role in projecting an association's image and message. Likewise, with the technological advances of the past decade, more people are doing research and purchasing via the World Wide Web. This, in turn, has expanded the resources available to membership marketing professionals by enabling them to reach a prospective member population they may not have been able to reach before.

Exhibit Booths

Exhibit booths are another form of marketing material that reaches out to potential members and enables them to ask questions regarding membership or member services. Exhibit booths staffed with knowledgeable employees or volunteers can be useful in both recruitment and retention. Because it is a large and costly marketing tool, it is important to design it wisely, keeping in mind all the issues that have been previously discussed.

There is a variety of exhibit equipment available to meet your budget and needs. Susan Friedmann, in *Tips & Techniques for Exhibiting Success,* offers cost-cutting tips for planning your display:

- Buy a display that:
    - packs compactly to save on storage
    - is lightweight to save on shipping
    - is portable to transport by auto, via delivery services, or as airline luggage
    - can be quickly and easily set up by your staff
    - adapts easily to different spaces by adding or removing components

- Use detachable graphics on a fabric background for maximum flexibility.

- Use heavy-duty laminated photo panels for more permanency if you want to change graphics often.

- Have someone proofread your copy to avoid change charges.

- Order your display graphics at least three weeks before the shipment date for the event to avoid overtime or rush charges.

- Give your exhibit representative camera-ready artwork to save on production cost.

- Buy your own carpet instead of renting, but be aware that, with shipment and upkeep costs, this may not be a cost savings.

- Buy your own plants to decorate the display. Silk plants are more durable.

- Order services early to avoid extra charges.

- Use the display for other purposes. Depending on space, you could use an exhibit booth as a resource center for members in the area or for display when your board of directors visits the office.

Techno-marketing

For lack of a better term, techno-marketing encompasses all forms of technology in getting the word out to prospective members, potential buyers, and members. Simply put, it is marketing through the use of technology. Ever since the boom of the World Wide Web there have been several books and classes on how to use it effectively. Techno-marketing includes, but is not limited to, the following.

Web sites. The Internet is currently the most commonly used research tool. If it can't be found on the Internet, it probably doesn't exist. Because of that belief, almost every provider of products and services has a Web site. A good Web site also should be easy to access by all types of computers and connections. Keep the graphics simple.

The Web site should answer these membership questions:

- How do I join?
- What is the cost of membership?
- What are the membership procedures?
- Can I enroll online, and is it secure?
- Whom do I contact?
- What do I get for my money?
- Why would I want to join?

When designing or updating your Web site, keep in mind these different technologies:

- Java™—mini-applications or programs
- Shockwave™—multimedia embedded movies
- RealAudio™—audio in real time
- Web chat—interactive group chats
- Password protection—especially useful for associations that don't want nonmembers to gain access to all materials posted on the Web site.
- Encrypted e-mail and page entry—allows credit card information or other data to be securely transmitted directly to the association.
- Listserves—topic-related group communication via audio and/or video; there are two ways to manage a listserve.

1. moderated—a moderator or listserve administrator reads and approves all items before posting. This is generally a slow process and can deter members who need quick answers.
2. unmoderated—the moderator or listserve administrator acts only to add or delete members from the list. This management promotes free and quick dialog among members. The administrator can occasionally monitor messages to make sure everyone is using proper listserve etiquette. To avoid liability based on listserve discussion, associations should post a disclaimer in the e-mail that welcomes new members to the listserve and gives them the general rules. Typically, such disclaimers start with, "The XYZ Association is not responsible for the messages posted on this listserve and only provides a forum for members to share information…."

- CD-ROM—Guided tours of the products and services of an association can be delivered via CD-ROM. It can be used in conjunction with a Web site to take the viewer to places with one click of a hotlink. It is an inexpensive way to transport a large amount of information and can use interactive technologies. Beware of using this as your sole medium of information because you may exclude a potential member group from joining.

- E-mail—Because e-mail is quick and inexpensive, it is commonly used in business. It is a great way to keep members up to date on current happenings and can be used as a membership and retention tool. Before relying solely on e-mail communication, you should poll your members and ask how they prefer to receive information. Just like regular mail, you don't want to overload your members' e-mail boxes. The same rules of direct mail apply: Entice your reader in the first few seconds, use your subject line wisely, and remember it's easier for someone to delete an e-mail than it is for him or her to throw away a direct mail piece.

As global as the Internet is becoming, it's important not to alienate any particular group that may not have access to the Internet. There are still many parts of the world and economic classes of potential members who don't have easy Internet access. Do not exclude these potential members from the information you provide.

Putting It All Together

All of these theories should work hand in hand with the development of new membership marketing materials. New collateral cannot be created in a vacuum, nor can an association present an appropriate image with unrelated materials. Communication is the most important way to maintain a consistent and effective message throughout your organization. Membership is everyone's job. Employees should buy into an image, remain consistent with style, and work together to increase membership. If collateral materials support the mission and image of the association, are delivered effectively, and are creative, you should have positive results.

RESOURCES

Ambler, Tim. *Marketing from Advertising to Zen.* London, England: Pitman Publishing, 1996.

Bacon, Mark S. *Do-It-Yourself Direct Marketing.* New York: John Wiley & Sons, Inc., 1997.

Beckwith, Harry. *Selling the Invisible,* New York: Warner Books, Inc., 1997.

Decker, Sam. *301 Do-It-Yourself Marketing Ideas.* Boston: Goldhirsh Group, Inc., 1997.

Ellsworth, Jill H., and Matthew V. Ellsworth. *Marketing on the Internet.* New York: John Wiley & Sons, Inc., 1997.

Friedmann, Susan A. *Tips & Techniques for Exhibiting Success.* Menlo Park, Calif.: Crisp Publications, Inc., 1995.

Maas, Jane. *Better Brochures, Catalogs and Mailing Pieces.* New York: St. Martin's Press, 1981.

Marconi, Joe. *Image Marketing.* Chicago: American Marketing Association, 1997.

Toffler, Betsy-Ann, and Jane Imber. *Dictionary of Marketing Terms.* Hauppauge, N.Y.: Barron's Educational Series, Inc., 1994.

Jamie Lee DeSimone is membership coordinator for the National Association of Independent Schools (NAIS). Her accomplishments include launching the association's first-ever direct mail campaign, redesigning all NAIS membership marketing materials, developing a traveling outreach program for the entire association, and achieving a 25 percent increase in new members since 1997. Before joining NAIS in 1995, DeSimone was Visa coordinator for the Transportation Federal Credit Union (TFCU) in Washington, D.C. While at TFCU, she was in charge of the marketing and management of its Visa credit card program and achieved a 300 percent increase in new accounts. DeSimone earned her bachelor's degree in Psychology in 1988 from the University of Pittsburgh.

About ASAE Publications

The American Society of Association Executives in Washington, DC, is an individual membership organization made up of more than 25,000 association executives and suppliers. Its members manage leading trade associations, individual membership societies, and voluntary organizations across the United States and in 44 countries around the globe. It also represents suppliers of products and services to the association community.

This book is one of the hundreds of titles available through the ASAE Bookstore. ASAE publications keep you a step ahead by providing you and your staff with valuable information resources for executive management, finance, human resources, membership, career management, fundraising, and technology.

A complete catalog of titles is available on the ASAE Web site at **www.asaenet.org** or call the Member Service Center at (202) 371-0940 for the latest printed catalog.

asae | american society of association executives

www.asaenet.org

Related Resources from ASAE

To order ASAE publications, visit the online bookstore at
www.asaenet.org/bookstore or contact the ASAE Member Service
Center by phone (202) 371-0940 or fax (202) 371-8315.

Allegiance: Fulfilling the Promise of One-to-One Marketing for Associations
By Dale G. Paulson

Why do members write you a check? The number of reasons is surprisingly limited, and by using the Allegiance program you'll capture a code for each member that will form the basis of your relationship. The system is easy to implement and requires no special software programs or elaborate mathematical formulas.

1998 • 78 pages • softcover • ISBN 0-88034-139-4
Product # LST-216790

Associations and the Global Marketplace: Profiles of Success
By Kimberly Svevo-Cianci

Learn how to expand memberships internationally, reach broader markets for conferences and trade shows, increase participation through affiliates and chapters, sell publication subscriptions worldwide, and reach additional users of networked databases and global information services. Each of the case studies tells of an association's experience in meeting the challenges of entering the global marketplace.

1995 • 353 pages • softcover • ISBN 0-88034-092-4
Product # LST-216525

Association Dues
ASAE Background Kit

A solid overview of planning, setting, and managing membership dues as a primary source of association income. Topics include dues structures, accounting for dues income, legal and tax issues, and handling a dues increase. Supplemented with sample documents and benchmarking statistics.

1999 • 144 pages • spiralbound
Product # LST-121015

Other Books from ASAE

Budgeting and Financial Management Handbook for Not-for-Profit Organizations

By Edward J. McMillan, CPA, CAE

Update an obsolete or ineffective budgeting system with a budgeting system that works. McMillan's "Continuous Budgeting" and financial management program is easy to implement and monitor. The book includes sample forms and financial statements, formats for sending budget documents to your approving body, and methods for addressing budget problems.

2000 • 128 pages • softcover • ISBN 0-88034-158-0
Product # LST-216722

The Extraordinary CEO

By Douglas C. Eadie

The "business" of being a CEO is what's left out of most texts on association management. Now in this insightful book, you have a resource that goes beyond mastering the skills required to conduct your association's day-to-day business. *The Extraordinary CEO* lifts you out of the fray to examine how you can diversify and enrich your portfolio of CEO leadership goals, skills, and attributes.

1999 • 96 pages • hardcover • ISBN 0-88034-156-4
Product # LST-216792

Strategic Alliances for Nonprofit Organizations

By Charles E. Bartling, CAE

Bartling uncovers why associations form alliances; what kinds of partnerships associations develop; how to find prospective partners and structure a deal that works; how to avoid the pitfalls of partnerships; how to maintain an effective, ongoing relationship; and how to end the alliance amicably when it no longer serves a worthwhile purpose.

1998 • 93 pages • softcover • ISBN 0-88034-143-2
Product # LST-216760

Other Books from ASAE

To order ASAE publications, visit the online bookstore at
www.asaenet.org/bookstore or contact the ASAE Member Service
Center by phone (202) 371-0940 or fax (202) 371-8315.

Millennium Membership:
How to Attract and Keep Members in the New Marketplace
By Mark Levin, CAE

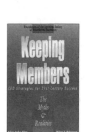

The needs and expectations of your members are changing
fast. *Millennium Membership* guides you through the steps
you must take to attract and keep members. Topics include
investing in technology, branding, and moving from mass
marketing to mass customization.

2000 • 154 pages • softcover • ISBN 0-88034-163-7
Product # LST-216812

Keeping Members: The Myths and Realities
By Arlene Farber Sirkin and Michael McDermott

Are you recruiting for retention or just one year? *Keeping
Members* redefines membership as the core business for associations and other nonprofit organizations. The authors dispel
12 popular myths about retention and reveal key strategies
for growth, focusing on how CEOs, staff, and volunteers each
have key roles to play in recruiting and keeping members.

1995 • ASAE Foundation • 125 pages • softcover • ISBN 0-88034-099-01
Product #: LST-213551

The National-Chapter Partnership:
A Guide for the Chapter Relations Professional
Edited by James DeLizia

Written for and by chapter relations professionals, this guide
will help you strengthen your national-chapter partnerships.
Each chapter includes a self-assessment for building your
chapter relations program. Ideas are generously illustrated
with samples from other associations. Contents include: The Organization of
Association Chapters. Legal and Tax Considerations. Empowering Chapters
Through Effective Communications. Membership Development. Implementing Government Relations Programs at the Chapter Level. Developing
New Chapters. The Chapter Relations Professional.

1993 • 335 pages • spiralbound • ISBN 0-88034-058-4
Product #: LST-217172